Dead Man

**Jonathan
Rosenbaum**

 Publishing

First published in 2000 by the
British Film Institute
21 Stephen Street, London W1P 2LN

Reprinted 2001

The British Film Institute promotes greater
understanding and appreciation of,
and access to, film and moving image
culture in the UK

Series design by Andrew Barron &
Collis Clements Associates

Typeset in Italian Garamond and Swiss 721BT
by D R Bungay Associates, Burghfield, Berks

Printed in Great Britain by
Norwich Colour Print, Drayton, Norfolk

British Library Cataloguing-in-Publication Data
A catalogue record for this book is available
from the British Library
ISBN 0-85170-806-4

Contents

Acknowledgments

A lot of people have helped me with this study – starting with Jim
Jarmusch, who has been especially generous with his time and resources,
and also including Lisa Alspector, Raymond Bellour, Nicole Brenez, Sara
Driver, Vanalyne Green, Tom Gunning, Ludvig Hertzberg, Alexander
Horwath, Kent Jones, Bill Krohn, Adrian Martin, Gregg Rickman, Peter
Thompson, Todd J. Tubutis and Rob White (who proposed that I write
this book in the first place). My thanks to all of them.

    I've borrowed a great deal from two previously published articles of
mine – 'Acid Western' (*Chicago Reader*, 28 June 1996) and 'A Gun Up Your
Ass: An Interview with Jim Jarmusch' (*Cineaste* vol. 22 no. 2, 1996,
pp. 20–3) – though all the material I've used has been substantially
reconfigured. For their various forms of help with the original versions of
these pieces, I'd like to thank the editors I've worked with on both
publications, in particular Alison True and Gary Crowdus.

1 Jim Jarmusch as American Independent, *Dead Man* as Deal-breaker

I

There isn't much agreement about when the post-Western succeeded the Western in American movies. Some might date the end of the traditional Western around 1962, the year in which both *The Man Who Shot Liberty Valance* and *Ride the High Country* appeared; others might think of 1969 (*The Wild Bunch*), 1970 (*Little Big Man* and *El topo*), 1971 (*McCabe and Mrs. Miller* and *The Last Movie*), 1972 (*Ulzana's Raid*), or 1973 (*Pat Garrett and Billy the Kid*). The point at which the post-Western sprang into being is even more difficult to determine. There are virtually as many dates as there are entries in this subgenre, because no two commentators can agree on what a post-Western is or should be.

So it shouldn't be too surprising that a post-Western as important as *Dead Man* had a fairly mixed as well as puzzled reception in the US when it came out in 1996, among critics as well as general audiences. One good friend, an academic who loves Westerns, told me that as an anti-Western along the lines of *Little Big Man*, Jim Jarmusch's film seemed all too familiar. Another esteemed colleague, a mainstream critic, told me that after an interesting opening sequence, the movie bored him to distraction. Roger Ebert, probably the most influential film reviewer in the US, accorded *Dead Man* one and a half stars in his review and concluded, 'Jim Jarmusch is trying to get at something here, and I don't have a clue what it is.' His review began, 'I once traveled for two days from Windhoek to Swakopmund through the Kalahari Desert, on a train without air conditioning, sleeping at night on a hard leather bench that swung down from the ceiling. That journey seemed a little shorter than the one that opens *Dead Man*.'[1]

The train journey opening *Dead Man* actually runs a little less than eight and a half minutes. In fairness to Ebert, this stretch is more aggressively eccentric and abrasive – in terms of pacing, rhythm, narrative discontinuity, behaviour and dialogue – than anything preceding it in Jarmusch's work, offering fair warning that viewers expecting the writer-director to behave on this occasion like a charming and lightweight raconteur will be in for a bumpy ride. Among the more unnerving aspects are the opening epigraph from Henri Michaux ('It is preferable not to travel with a dead man'),[2] and an anything-but-tuneful employment of Neil Young's guitar that is closer to a rhythmic sound effect than to any sort of recognisable melody. Then there is a sinister shift in passengers over various time breaks marked by fade-outs and fade-ins from city slickness to barbarism as mid-western accountant William Blake (Johnny Depp) proceeds west, and escalating examples of meanness over the same evolution. When the train's fireman (Crispin Glover) suddenly seats himself across from Blake and assertively engages him in conversation, he begins with a surrealist monologue (reproduced at the beginning of the Appendix) that comes out of left field, then starts firing personal questions and comments at Blake about his destination and background that include the suggestion that he's heading both for hell and his own grave, culminating in this stretch of gratuitous unpleasantness:

Blake and the fireman

FIREMAN

Wife?

BLAKE

No.

FIREMAN

Fiancée?

BLAKE

I had one of those, but she changed her mind.

FIREMAN
(*speculating*)

She found herself somebody else.

BLAKE
(*defensively*)

No.

FIREMAN
(*gruffly insisting, as if to himself*)

She did.

This exchange is succeeded by explosions of gunfire as many of Blake's fellow passengers start firing out the train windows at buffaloes; over a million of them, the fireman informs us, were slaughtered in the previous year. And once Blake arrives at the town of Machine, immediately after the opening credits, things only get creepier, more ornery and disorienting. The following detail from the script, just after Blake steps off the train,

Shooting buffalo

Arriving in Machine

probably derived from Jarmusch's research, isn't in the film. But it wouldn't have been out of place if Jarmusch had managed to include it, because it sets the tone of literal contrariness that characterises the film as a whole:

BLAKE looks around him in a daze. The town has no train depot, but instead a strange wooden platform; a crude wooden turntable with railroad tracks across it.

As soon as BLAKE is several yards away from the train, scruffy, drunken-looking men appear out of nowhere, and begin to turn the train platform around, pointing the locomotive in the opposite direction.

II

In the interests of full disclosure, I should note that I've been friends with Jarmusch for the past seventeen years, though I haven't been an unqualified supporter of his work as a whole. I published a brief and somewhat mixed review of *Permanent Vacation* (1980) in a New York weekly (the long-defunct *Soho News*) before we ever met, and when I first got to know him, his main identity for me was as the boyfriend of Sara Driver, a film-maker I was writing a chapter about for a survey of independent and experimental cinema called *Film: The Front Line 1983*. Once Jarmusch began to become famous with *Stranger Than Paradise* (1984), I followed his career with sympathetic interest, and when I was asked to interview him about his third feature, *Down by Law* (1986), for

Cahiers du Cinéma, I was happy to oblige. But over the course of his next two features, *Mystery Train* (1989) and *Night on Earth* (1992), my growing fascination with some of his formal and thematic preoccupations was somewhat qualified by an overall sense that he was coasting, adopting the role of a sophisticated urban entertainer without significantly expanding his talents or in some cases adequately exploring his territory. (I was bothered, for instance, by the way some of the black Memphis characters in *Mystery Train* sounded more like New Yorkers to me than southerners.) Although I respected him for the ways in which he fiercely maintained his independence – despite numerous offers and opportunities to work for the Hollywood studios and join the mainstream – he seemed to have etched out a narrow if comfortable niche for himself that didn't suggest many surprises or provocative future developments.

Dead Man changed all that. It represented both a quantum leap and, at the same time, a logical step in relation to Jarmusch's earlier work. That is, without fundamentally betraying the thrust of his previous features, he also offered a series of new challenges to his audience in relation to form as well as content. Without quite contradicting the minimalism that had informed his style in the previous films, he had broadened his canvas to take in a lot more.

Part of this undoubtedly came from a radical change in tone; as Greil Marcus overstates it somewhat in his rousing defence of the film in the online magazine *Salon*, 'There is no hint in Jim Jarmusch's previous work that he was interested in anything but irony, and this movie has no irony.'[3] And more recently, Jarmusch's subsequent feature, *Ghost Dog: The Way of the Samurai* (1999), has shown that *Dead Man* brought about a substantial shift in his overall ambitions. An overall sense of tragedy permeating *Ghost Dog* is part of what might be termed the *Dead Man* legacy, along with a deeply felt relationship between the present and the historical past. More specifically, there's the brief reappearance of Gary Farmer as Nobody, saying 'Stupid fucking white man', and another scene involving the hero's retribution against a pair of deer hunters – a scene that Jarmusch himself admitted to me could easily have turned up in *Dead Man*.

One reason why I've chosen to include a lot of interview material in
this book is that Jarmusch is unusually articulate about his positions and
strategies, and in most respects his views of *Dead Man* are compatible with
my own. But in some cases our views are different, and I've also wanted to
juxtapose and challenge some of my own pet theories about the film (such
as my reading of its treatment of violence) with his own somewhat
different responses – not because I necessarily think that he's right and
I'm wrong, or vice versa ('writing' and 'reading' strategies aren't always
identical, in any case, nor should they be), but because I'd like to offer the
reader certain choices.

III
**Y'now, it's funny. You come to someplace new and everything looks
just the same.**
Eddie (Richard Edson) in *Stranger Than Paradise*

After his second feature, *Stranger Than Paradise*, made him an international
name, Jarmusch seemed at the height of arthouse fashion. Having already
slightly known him, I could tell that the extent to which he suddenly
became a figurehead for the American independent cinema bemused him
in certain ways. Given the aura of hip, glamorous downtown Manhattan
culture that seemed to follow him everywhere he went, how could it not? I
can still recall a *New York Times* profile several years ago that was so
entranced by his romantic image that it suggested that, simply because
Jarmusch chose to live in the Bowery, that neighbourhood automatically
took on magical, transcendent properties. In contrast to a much more
embattled *and* political American independent such as Jon Jost, Jarmusch
had (partly unwittingly) become the chief means of the media in
glamorising and indeed 'selling' the American independent cinema from
the mid-80s onward.

Consistently rejecting all Hollywood offers (echoed in the response
of Los Angeles taxi driver Winona Ryder to showbiz agent Gena Rowlands
in the first episode of *Night on Earth*), Jarmusch cultivated a stylish
international arthouse reputation by acting in the films of such friends as

Alex Cox, Robert Frank, Raúl Ruiz, the Kaurismaki brothers and Billy Bob Thornton – creating a certain model for independence that combined the conviviality of the French New Wave with some of the down-home brashness of storefront theatre. The combination of his white hair and his all-black clothes made him immediately recognisable as a figure. And thanks in part to the influence of New York minimalism, his career has managed an exemplary combination of experimentation and repetition, striking an even balance between business savvy and artistic self-preservation. Moreover, he's spiced the spare decorum of New York minimalism with the unruly, diverse charm of various 'foreign' and ethnic points of view. Investing most of his energy in character rather than story, he returns repeatedly to the notion of looking at the same thing in different ways – or looking at different things the same way.

   Permanent Vacation, *Stranger Than Paradise* and *Down by Law* are all 'road movies' of a sort, featuring music by John Lurie and strategic pauses in the dialogue. Yet each is a different form of road movie, with a different sort of Lurie music and even a different kind of silence, formally articulated in a different manner. *Stranger Than Paradise* and *Down by Law* follow two Americans and an unassimilated European wandering through a changing black-and-white landscape that obstinately remains the same. Yet few performances can be more dissimilar than those of Ezster Balint and Roberto Benigni; and the three locations in *Stranger Than Paradise*, shot by Tom DiCillo (New York, Cleveland, Florida), are worlds apart from those in Louisiana – New Orleans, prison, swamp and forest, shot by Robby Müller – in *Down by Law*. (The look of the latter film, and Müller's influence in general, would ultimately prove to be the more decisive; Müller has in fact shot all of Jarmusch's subsequent features with the exception of *Night on Earth*, shot by Frederick Elmes.)

   The three-part construction of these two features carries over into *Mystery Train*, though here the time frame (one twenty-four-hour stretch) and locations (a few dilapidated blocks in Memphis) remain the same in all three sections while the central characters are different. And in *Night on Earth*, in which Jarmusch moved from a three-part sketch film to a five-part sketch film, devoted to five taxi drivers across the globe and their passengers, he retained the simultaneity of *Mystery Train* while altering its meaning by assigning four of the five sketches to different time zones.

Despite their formal ingenuity and various charms, *Mystery Train* and *Night on Earth* both indicated that Jarmusch was paving something of a rut for himself as a minimalist entertainer and downtown-Manhattan mannerist. Though these films weren't by any means devoid of thematic interest – for starters, both are preoccupied with death, anticipating *Dead Man* and recalling the shot of a hearse that opens *Down by Law* – they carried out their limited game plans a little too neatly. One felt Jarmusch was capable of more but hadn't yet found the nerve to risk losing his constituency by pursuing it. Yet once he found the nerve, it became much easier to see why he had hesitated before making *Dead Man* – a project he had been mulling over for years. Its first incarnation, around 1990, was as a Western to be shot in a 'scope format called *Ghost Dog*, a title eventually given to Jarmusch's subsequent feature. Starting off as a collaboration with novelist and screenwriter Rudy Wurlitzer, the project quickly fell aground over disagreements about Wurlitzer's script, sadly terminating the friendship between the two, and Jarmusch turned next to *Night on Earth*, which he wrote alone, returning to *Dead Man* as a solo venture only after that sketch film was completed.

When it premiered at Cannes in 1995, it suddenly became apparent that Jarmusch's honeymoon with the American press was over – although his international reputation had survived intact. (As more recent proof of the latter, when I was in Japan in December 1999, shortly after the release there of *Ghost Dog*, I was fascinated to discover how prominently displayed the videos for Jarmusch's early features were in the shops I visited in Tokyo, Kyoto and Hiroshima – during which time *Stranger Than Paradise*, fifteen years after its initial release, was listed as a best-seller, in the top ten.)

There are multiple reasons for Jarmusch's altered American profile, including changing fashions and succeeding generational tastes. But it's worth considering at the outset what has happened to the American independent cinema over those same fifteen years, which has a lot to do with Jarmusch's changed position in the media. When thinking about today's ambitious American film-makers, one of the easiest ways to distinguish between Hollywood employees (current or prospective) and those with more creative freedom is to look for logical and consistent developments from one film to the next – a clear line of concerns that runs beyond fads and market developments. Though it's possible to see a director such as Alfred Hitchcock developing certain formal and thematic ideas in his 50s movies, there's little likelihood of such an evolution being possible for a studio director today, what with agent packages, script bids, multiple rewrites, stars who get script approval and/or say over the final cut, test marketing and so on. Within such a context, it's significant that Jarmusch as a writer-director, virtually alone among American independents who make narrative features that get mainstream exposure, owns the negatives of all his films. This means that, for better and for worse, all the developments – and non-developments – that have taken place in his work between *Permanent Vacation* and *Ghost Dog* are of his own making.

This provides one model of American independent film-making, but not the one that most of the media are presently preoccupied with. Their model tends to gravitate around the Sundance festival, where success in the independent sector is typically defined as landing a big-time distributor and/or a studio contract – the exposure, in short, that goes hand in glove with dependence on large institutional backing, hence loss of independence. And though it would be wrong to assume that Jarmusch isn't himself dependent on such forces to get his films into theatres (*Dead Man* was distributed in the US by Miramax), the salient difference between him and most other independents is that he's strong enough to afford the luxury of brooking no creative interference when it comes to making production and post-production decisions.

By the time *Dead Man* appeared, the popular notion of American independent film-making had largely shifted from the paradigm represented by Jarmusch to the murkier model of Quentin Tarantino – a film-maker who has never owned the negatives, much less had final cut, on any of his features. The role played by Miramax in this shift is of course crucial, and not only because Miramax has distributed *Dead Man* as well as Tarantino's features, so some consideration of this hands-on distributor and its flair for promotion is crucial to understanding the altered public perception of 'independence'.

Dead Man was trimmed by fourteen minutes after its Cannes premiere – without serious injury, in my opinion – but all of this recutting was done by Jarmusch, without Miramax's input. And despite the expressed desire of Miramax's Harvey Weinstein to make further cuts prior to the film's release, Jarmusch was contractually protected from any such interference. By contrast, Tarantino has welcomed Miramax into his cutting room and relinquished final control over his work for the sake of the distributor's full support. He's even been rewarded for his co-operation with his own distribution subsidiary at Miramax, Rolling Thunder, whose first two releases were *Chungking Express* (1994) and *Switchblade Sisters* (1974).

Jarmusch, on the other hand, appearing at the New York Film Critics Circle's annual awards to accept a prize for Müller's cinematography on *Dead Man*, publicly blamed Miramax for the relatively disappointing performance of *Dead Man* at the American box-office, and has implied elsewhere that his refusal to re-edit the film led to a relatively indifferent promotion of the film. (Within my own experience, one prominent programmer planning a Jarmusch retrospective that year told me that, when he requested a print of *Dead Man*, he was informed, 'You don't want to show that, it's a dog' – or words to that effect.)

With the help of unabashed Sundance and Miramax supporters in the press – journalists eager to promote film as a business over film as an art, and therefore ready to place the future of cinema in the hands of agents and producers rather than artists – the popular model for so-called American independence has in effect passed from Jarmusch's freedom to Tarantino's servitude. Certainly the uncritical way in which most of the American mainstream press has rubber-stamped the major decisions of Miramax – ignoring the features that they pick up for distribution but fail to release or make available to most markets (a list that has already included major works by Jacques Demy, Abbas Kiarostami and Jacques

Tati, among others), overlooking the meddlesome changes they've frequently made to features (in some cases ruinously, in my opinion, as with Chen Kaige's *Temptress Moon* [1996]), and even quoting with approval and much fanfare Harvey Weinstein's criticism of the main selections and prizes at the Cannes Film Festival in 1999[4] – has fostered such an impression.

Much as I liked *Dead Man* when I first saw it at the Cannes premiere, it wasn't until after I'd seen it a few more times that I began to appreciate it in any depth. By the time it opened belatedly in the US, in 1996 – long after runs in most other countries, including Australia and Turkey, a delay reportedly caused in part by Miramax's lack of enthusiasm for the film after Jarmusch refused to recut – it had become something of a cause for me, not to mention a kind of semiconscious litmus test that I imposed on others. After I successfully proposed interviewing Jarmusch about the film for *Artforum*, the assignment got cancelled in favour of a feature by someone else on *I Shot Andy Warhol* (1996) for the same issue, so I arranged to do the interview with Jarmusch for *Cineaste*. (Portions of both that phone interview – conducted in April – and a more recent one, conducted in November 1999 and previously unpublished, are to be found throughout this book.) Then, towards the end of the year, I received a request from *Artforum* that I send them my take on 'the best and worst' of 1996, cinematically speaking – an annual symposium that I'd contributed to the previous year. I impulsively replied, 'The best: *Dead Man* is released in the US. The worst: *Artforum* decides that *I Shot Andy Warhol* is more important.' I'd mistakenly assumed that *Artforum*'s editors would run my rude reply, and another three years were to pass before I was asked again to contribute to another annual survey in the magazine.

In other words, *Dead Man* might be described as something of a deal-breaker, and not only for me. For Jarmusch, it marked a decisive change in his stateside profile – partially, I think, because it was the first film in his career to have direct political overtones and implications. Of what kind? Some viewers might simply say that the film is anti-American, but to claim even this much already presupposes a definition of what America itself is that the film implicitly challenges.

More precisely, I would define the political and ideological singularity of *Dead Man* in two ways: that it is the first Western made by a white film-maker that assumes as well as addresses Native American spectators, and that it offers one of the ugliest portrayals of white American capitalism to be found in American movies. On the surface, the former distinction may appear to be a modest or incidental difference, but I believe it to be a profound and far-reaching one that affects practically everything else one might say about the film, morally and politically as well as historically. For the same reason, I regard it as both the linchpin of this study and what makes it, along with its portrayal of capitalism, a conclusive 'deal-breaker' for a certain number of white viewers, even though many of them may be completely unaware of this fact – and despite the fact that I'm speaking more of existential intent than of anything else. These two political factors come together in a manner best described by Kent Jones:

In Jim Jarmusch's *Dead Man*, there is no American West. There is only a landscape that America the conqueror has emptied of its natives and turned into a capitalist charnel house. The Western is the American cinema's pride and joy as well as its good will ambassador, and the alleged acuity with which it reflects what's going on in American society has been an urgent topic for sociologically minded critics and 'genre theorists'. Even during its fallow periods (early Thirties, late Seventies through Eighties), there has been a persistent desire to track its shifting configurations as if it were a State of the Union address. But even during the heyday of the 'anti-Western' (the term itself is a sign of how deeply the genre is embedded in our consciousness), there was nothing as bluntly dismissive of the United States of America's very existence as Jarmusch's cinematic poem of embitterment.[5]

Any film proposing a redefinition of the film audience has to be considered radical to some degree, though it might be argued that Jarmusch has been carrying out a programme of this kind since the early stages of his career – at the very least since *Stranger Than Paradise*. The difference between that film and *Dead Man* in terms of redefining an audience may not seem very substantial to most people outside the US, but I think it's worthy of some careful attention. Broadly speaking, *Stranger Than Paradise* redefined the hip and stylish audience of the 80s in international terms, by presenting how New York, suburban Ohio and rural Florida looked to a Hungarian teenager (Ezster Balint) *and* how a Hungarian teenager looked to a couple of New Yorkers (John Lurie and Richard Edson). Historically speaking, this was a move in direct opposition to the more xenophobic assumptions about the movie audience that many other American independents had at the time and still have today – which were in fact the kind of workaday assumptions already reflected in Pauline Kael's divisions between French and American spectators as 'them' and 'us' twenty years earlier (notably in her famous essay on *Bonnie and Clyde*, but also in many of her other writings as well, and subsequently in the criticism of most of her disciples).[6] Around the time that *Dead Man* was released, Kevin Smith – the director of *Clerks* (1994) and *Mall Rats* (1995) and more recently *Chasing Amy* (1997) and *Dogma* (1999) – was quoted as saying, 'I don't feel that I have to go back and view European or other foreign films because I feel like these guys [i.e. Jarmusch and others] have already done it for me, and I'm getting it filtered through them. That ethic works for me.'[7] In short, one might postulate that the growing isolationism of some Americans, as reflected in Smith's remark, has made *Dead Man* an even more radical gesture today than it might have been fifteen, twenty or thirty years ago.

After showing us New York, Cleveland and rural Florida through the eyes of a Hungarian, Jarmusch then presented New Orleans and the wilds of Louisiana through the eyes of an Italian (Roberto Benigni in *Down by Law*), and Memphis and its rock shrines through the eyes of a Japanese couple (Masatoshi Nagase and Youki Kudoh in *Mystery Train*). Two films later, it is Gary Farmer's robust, charismatic Nobody, a Plains Indian who is half Blood and half Blackfoot, who plays the 'foreign' role in *Dead Man* – a fact touching on the scandal that Native Americans are treated in the United States as if they were foreigners. Indeed, *Dead Man* is one of the few Westerns to see through the cheesy mythology – irrational yet implicit in diverse aspects of American life and behaviour – that white people were the first 'real' or 'true' North American settlers, but I hasten to add that its approach to this issue is casual and poetic rather than preachy. The warm, comic friendship between Nobody and Blake, neither of whom entirely understands the other, is central to the film.

IV

A little bit of history may be useful at this point:

Without going into detail, and merely to give a general idea (even if we do not feel entirely justified in rounding off figures when it is a question of human lives), it will be recalled that in 1500 the world population is approximately 400 million, of whom 80 million inhabit the Americas. By the middle of the sixteenth century, out of these 80 million, there remain ten. Or limiting ourselves to Mexico: on the eve of the conquest, its population is about 25 million; in 1600, it is one million. If the word genocide has ever been applied to a situation with some accuracy, this is here the case. It constitutes a record not only in relative terms (a destruction in the order of 90 percent or more), but also in absolute

A strange friendship

terms, since we are speaking of a population diminution estimated at 70 million human lives. None of the great massacres of the twentieth century can be compared to this hecatomb. [8]

Tzvetan Todorov, writing in *The Conquest of America*, goes on to express the possible objection that 'there is no point in attempting to establish responsibilities, or even to speak of genocide rather than of a natural catastrophe,' stressing that the number of Indians who were directly murdered, 'during the wars or outside of them', was relatively small, those who were badly treated was slightly higher, and those who died by diseases ('by "microbe shock"') were clearly in the majority. Nevertheless, even if the issue of responsibility is obfuscated somewhat by the figures, the immensity of the genocide – and genocide still strikes me as being the appropriate term, despite Todorov's cautious second thoughts – remains so staggering that it might be said that white racism against Indians, in contrast to racism against Jews, blacks and Asians, has been qualitatively as well as quantitatively different, most of all in the scant degree to which it has been acknowledged. One might go further and say that, Ralph Ellison's *Invisible Man* to the contrary, it is perhaps Native Americans and not African Americans who are most invisible in American life.

If America – the continent of America, in Todorov's terms – is haunted by the genocide that presided over its conquest, one thing that makes *Dead Man* a haunted film is a sense of this enormity crawling around its edges, informing every moment and every gesture, without ever quite taking centre stage. This makes it all the more appropriate that its title character is played by Johnny Depp, one of the most haunted beautiful actors in American movies – a presence whose brooding quietness and mystery suggest Buster Keaton.

For even though Depp is called upon to play an archetypal white man with the name of an archetypal English poet, it is worth noting that the actor had a grandfather who was a Cherokee Indian whom he felt very close to as a young child. (He died when Depp was seven, and although of course we never see this in the film, an Indian man with a full head-dress is tattooed on one of Depp's forearms.)[9]

Depp's brooding
stillness

Buster Keaton in
Go West (1925)

ROSENBAUM (at the time of the film's US premiere): How many Native
   Americans have seen *Dead Man* so far?

JARMUSCH: At this point very few. But it's going to show in Taos, and I know
   there's a big Native American contingency that goes there. Gary Farmer's
   having a benefit in Canada, and I'm going to take the film eventually to
   the Makah reservation to show them. And then Gary and I are going to
   make sure that videos are distributed to every reservation video store we
   can get them in. That's really important to us.

When I spoke to Jarmusch three years later about the same subject, he
could describe to me in greater detail the enthusiastic responses –

specifically, the whooping expressions of approval – he found in Native American audiences towards the film. He also noted their preference for the longer version of the film that was shown in Cannes – a version that still exists in a single print, with French subtitles.

ROSENBAUM: Why did you make Nobody half Blood as well as half Blackfoot?
JARMUSCH: Well, I wanted to situate him as a Plains Indian, so I chose those two tribes that did intermix at certain points historically but also were at war with each other. So his parents in my mind were like Romeo and Juliet; there was even a reference to that in the original script.

'I know of no white film that has tried to assume an Indian's point of view,' Tag Gallagher noted in a 1993 article.[10]

Perhaps the effort has always looked doomed to failure – and indecent. As Ford observes in *Cheyenne Autumn* (1964), it is white words, white language, that have been our most potent weapon against Indians. Are we, the descendants of their destroyers, now to presume to tell their stories in the language that destroyed them? Is it time, yet, to acknowledge the responsibility to make their stories part of their common heritage?

Given such a critical context, can *Dead Man* be regarded as either a failure or as indecent? I don't believe so, but in fairness to Gallagher, I don't believe it 'tries to assume an Indian's point of view', either. Perhaps more significantly, the film is treated with a great deal of respect by two Native American film scholars who have recently written at length about Native American representation in cinema, Ward Churchill and Jacquelyn Kilpatrick.[11] And the issue may finally be more a matter of ethics than one of politics – a question, indeed, of simple *politesse* more than political correctness.

ROSENBAUM: As I recall, none of the Native American dialogue is subtitled.
JARMUSCH: No, I didn't want it subtitled. I wanted it to be a little gift for those people who understand the language. Also, the joke about tobacco is for

Native American
presences

indigenous American people. I hope the last line, 'But Nobody, I don't
smoke,' will be like a hilarious joke to them: 'Oh man, this white man still
doesn't get it.' Makah was incredibly difficult; Gary [Farmer] had to learn
it phonetically and read it off big cards. Even the Makah people had
trouble, because it's a really complicated language.

ROSENBAUM: I've heard that Nobody speaks four languages in the film –
Blackfoot, Cree, Makah and English. How did you write the Indian
dialogue?

JARMUSCH: Well, Michelle Thrush, who's in the film, spoke Cree and is Cree.
We wrote some dialogue together and then she translated it with
someone else who was even more fluent.

In his extended essay 'Fantasies of the Master Race: The Cinematic
Colonization of American Indians', Churchill, a Keetoowah Cherokee,
begins with the assertion that 'The cinematic depiction of indigenous
peoples in America is objectively racist on all levels,'[12] and the fifty-seven

pages and 224 footnotes that follow back up this indictment with a great deal of plausible evidence. When it comes to considering the supposedly revisionist Westerns that allegedly rectify the distortions and abuses of other Westerns – films such as *Cheyenne Autumn*, *Little Big Man* and *Dances with Wolves* (1990) – Churchill is especially withering in his charges of hypocrisy and/or indifference to the facts. In her *Celluloid Indians: Native Americans and Film*, Kilpatrick, who is of Choctaw, Cherokee and Irish descent, considers films by as well as about Native Americans, and though her rhetoric is less angry than Churchill's, her observations generally prove to be no less critical.

Dead Man is singled out by Churchill as 'undoubtedly' the best of a handful of 'white-constructed' North American films defining 'a genuine break with convention in its handling of Indian themes'. He also calls it 'a well-crafted and accessibly surrealistic black & white travelogue across late nineteenth-century North America, replete with biting literary metaphors and analogies to contemporary circumstance'.[13] And Kilpatrick, who accords much more space to the film, virtually begins her discussion by calling it 'a very realistic film' and ends by noting, 'Whether one likes the film or not, there are a few undeniable facts about *Dead Man*, one of the most important of which is that Jarmusch's film shows a significant effort to depict a Native existence stripped of the stereotypes of the last hundred years of filmmaking. It is a very good start.'[14]

To both of these analysts, Gallagher might respond, following the argument of his 1993 essay, that 'Authenticity as a moral imperative is a recent obsession ... accorded relatively little importance during most of the last hundred thousand years, even (and especially) by historians,' because 'Authenticity was thought unachievable. And for good reason. The past, after all, does not exist, except in our individual imaginations, and no two of us can imagine even yesterday in the same way.'[15]

This is undoubtedly a point to be made and reckoned with. It might be argued, indeed, that *Dead Man*'s verisimilitude is only approximate at best. Yet if one approaches the issue of Native American representation more existentially, and specifically in relation to the Native American spectator, the issue might be conceptualised somewhat differently.

Responding to the question, 'What would (or might) a Native American spectator think of this representation of Native Americans?', the most likely answer in most cases would surely be, 'I never thought of that.' And the reason such a thought would not be entertained is that the *presence* of Native American spectators as part of American society and therefore as part of the American audience is seldom taken into account. The more habitual assumption is to imagine such spectators off in their respective reservations, removed from so-called American life. From this point of view, the existential innovation of Jarmusch, simple yet crucial, is to acknowledge that he inhabits the same universe as Native American spectators who might happen to see *Dead Man*: a modest gesture that proves to be a radical one only because apparently no one has ever made it before, at least not in the same way.

Nobody in the Makah settlement

2 The Story

I

The film opens with someone named William Blake (Johnny Depp), an accountant from Cleveland who has recently lost both his parents (who have died) and his fiancée (who has 'changed her mind'), travelling west on a train with the promise of a job at a metalworks in a town called Machine. He keeps dozing off and waking to new sets of fellow passengers, including several who fire their guns out the windows at a herd of buffalo.

ROSENBAUM: When Blake is travelling west on the train and sees other passengers firing at buffaloes, the fireman says 'a million were killed last year.' Was there a year in which that many were actually shot?
JARMUSCH: There was a period in the mid-1870s. I think in 1875 well over a million were shot and the government was very supportive of this being done, because, 'No buffalo, no Indians.' They were trying to get the railroad through and having a lot of problems with the Lakota and different tribes. I even have in a book somewhere an etching or engraving of a train passing through the Great Plains with a lot of guys even standing upright on the top of cars firing at these herds of buffalo, slaughtering them mindlessly.

When Blake arrives at his destination – a nightmarishly squalid settlement of festering pollution and nastiness – he's told derisively by both John Dickinson (Robert Mitchum), the blustering, hostile metalworks owner, and one of his curt employees, John Scholfield (John Hurt), that they no longer need an accountant, having filled the position some time ago. After repairing to a saloon to spend the remainder of his meagre supply of cash on a small bottle of whiskey, Blake runs into a former prostitute named Thel Russell (Mili Avital) selling paper flowers and winds up in bed with her. Later that night Thel's former lover, Charlie (Gabriel Byrne) – who, as we discover later, happens to be Dickinson's son – bursts in and, after a

Dickinson

Blake and Thel

Charlie

brief exchange with her, shoots her dead when she moves to shield Blake; the same bullet seriously wounds Blake in the chest. Grabbing Thel's bedside pistol, Blake fires back three times, eventually hitting his assailant in the neck and killing him. He then makes a clumsy getaway on Charlie Dickinson's pinto after falling out the window.

The next day in the woods we see Nobody (Gary Farmer) – a Native American outcast due to his 'mixed' parentage, half Blood (his mother) and half Blackfoot (his father) – trying without success to remove the bullet close to Blake's heart with a knife. Despite some mutual problems in understanding each other, they become riding companions. (Nobody, who as a boy was once taken as a prisoner to England, where he first encountered and became well versed in the poetry of William Blake, is convinced that this Blake is the poet himself; Blake, who's never heard of the poet, thinks that Nobody is crazy. After escaping from England, Nobody was labelled a liar, He Who Talks Loud Saying Nothing, and eventually expelled from his tribe.) Nobody guides Blake through the wilderness toward the northwest coast, in effect leading him toward his own death. As Nobody points out, because the bullet in Blake's chest can't be removed, he's already a dead man, and the remainder of the film is devoted to Blake's adjustment to this fact. (It may be the most protracted death scene in movies; by comparison, Garbo's death in *Camille* is a quickie.) In the meantime, Dickinson has dispatched three bounty hunters – Cole Wilson (Lance Henriksen), Conway Twill (Michael Wincott) and Johnny 'The Kid' Pickett (Eugene Byrd) – to bring Blake back dead or alive, and he later offers rewards to various other people.

Putting a price on Blake's head ensures plenty of skirmishes on his trek with Nobody towards the northwest, and Cole Wilson – the craziest of the bounty hunters, who reportedly 'fucked his parents', 'killed them', 'cooked them up' and 'ate them' – eventually kills both 'The Kid' and Conway, the latter of whom he also eats with relish. Meanwhile Blake himself, in order to survive, becomes a hardened killer; in one skirmish, with Nobody backing him up, he kills three murderous and sexually ambivalent trappers (Jared Harris, Billy Bob Thornton and Iggy Pop, the latter of whom wears a dress).

The bounty hunters

The corpse of 'The Kid'

The trappers

One night, Nobody ingests peyote, hallucinates that Blake has become a skeleton and, taking Blake's glasses, abandons him in the woods. Close to starvation, Blake has visions of his own, but successfully kills two marshals who are searching for him (named Lee and Marvin, in tribute to one of Jarmusch's favourite movie actors – who previously inspired him, John Lurie, and a few other friends to found a somewhat jokey yet reverent club, The Sons of Lee Marvin). Later, Blake curls up to sleep next to a slain fawn. He re-encounters Nobody one night while the latter is making love to an Indian woman (Michelle Thrush), and they resume their travel together. After Blake kills a racist missionary (Alfred Molina) at a trading post and gets wounded again by another bullet, they

The trading post

Heading for the coast

continue by canoe until they finally reach a Makah village on the Pacific coast, where Nobody arranges for Blake's death by negotiating for a canoe to send him off in to 'the other side'. As Blake drifts off in the canoe, Nobody is approached by Cole Wilson, and the two men immediately shoot and kill one another.

II

ROSENBAUM: A subjective impression I had when I first saw *Dead Man* at Cannes is that it's your first political film. The view of America is a lot darker than in your previous films.

JARMUSCH: I think it *is* a lot darker. You know, you can define everything as being political and analyse it politically. So I don't really know how to respond to that because it wasn't a conscious kind of proselytising. But I'm proud of the film because of the fact that on the surface it's a very simple story and a simple metaphor that the physical life is this journey that we take. And I wanted that simple story, and the relationship between these two guys from different cultures who are both loners and lost and for whatever reasons are completely disoriented from their cultures.

That's the story for me, that's what it's about. But at the same time, unlike my other films, the story invited me to have a lot of other themes that exist peripherally: violence, guns, American history, a sense of place, spirituality, William Blake and poetry, fame, outlaw status – all these things that are certainly part of the fabric of the film, that maybe unfortunately, at least for the distributors, work better when you've seen the film more than once. Because they're subtle and they're not intended to hit you over the head with a sledgehammer.

ROSENBAUM: Did *Dead Man* take a lot longer to shoot than your other films?

JARMUSCH: It took longer because of the company moves, and carrying all that equipment – horses and wardrobe – into areas where you can't see a phone wire. The actual shooting time was no more than on the others.

ROSENBAUM: Was it mainly the central states?

JARMUSCH: Yeah. All over Arizona, including soundstages in Phoenix, for the train and office interiors. We shot that little Western town out in the desert south of Phoenix. We also went to northern Arizona, outside of Flagstaff, where we shot those aspen forests where Nobody tells the story of his life, and then the black lava beds where he takes peyote. Then we shot the factory and some train stuff in Nevada. In southern Oregon we shot the trading post, we built and shot the Indian village, and did a few other things there. Then we went to northern California for the redwoods and the ocean. And we didn't fly, we drove everywhere. It was really hard – no time off for anything, except for when I got tickets for everyone to see Neil Young and Crazy Horse in Sedona, Arizona. That was the first time I ever got to meet Neil.

ROSENBAUM: Was *Dead Man* your most expensive film? Of course, on *Night on Earth* you had to travel around the world.

JARMUSCH: That was less than half the budget of *Dead Man*. On *Dead Man* it was the period stuff – the wardrobe, the horses, all the research, having the right guns, and all the moves. It should have been a twelve million dollar film, just on the small side, and it was more like nine. The line producer that I always work with refused to do the film for nine. But I couldn't get twelve because of the black and white, which is much more expensive to process now than colour. So we did it for nine, but it was hell. Yeah, it was our most expensive film; *Ghost Dog* was seven. But it really took a toll on everyone.

ROSENBAUM: Incidentally, why is that smoke that you see coming from the Dickinson Metalworks animated?

JARMUSCH: I wanted it to look more realistic, and I didn't have enough budget to do that matte shot to my satisfaction, so the smoke looked kind of cartoon-like. But I couldn't redo it and I didn't want to not have the smoke.

In fact, this smoke is the second use of animation in the film. The first is the opening credits, which enact their own form of death and dissolution.

3 On Tobacco

Sitting in the archives in Harare [Zimbabwe] now, poring over these musty documents, what seems most obvious is that it is the white man who is obsessed with tobacco, and indeed not without reason, because tobacco is crucially identified with the project of invasion and later colonialism. These early documents read as superb instances of projection, arcane evidence of the process by which tobacco – so closely identified with the savage – was to become the medium by which Rhodesia entered the international monetary community, was to become synonymous with white Rhodesia, with the colonial enterprise. [...]

I wonder what the picture will look like in a few centuries' time, how the picture of our culture will be configured. Who, I wonder, will be subject to mimetic mockery and caricature, where will projection be located? Will it be the smokers in their ghettos and glasshouses and underground lairs who seem to be so abject and socially irresponsible? Or will researchers of the everyday wonder, in the future, why so much scorn was heaped on tobacco smoking in the fin de siècle, why this quotidian habit attracted so much moral vehemence. What was at stake, they might wonder, in these intricate patterns of projection?

Lesley Stern[16]

The most elaborate running gag in *Dead Man*, occurring in one form or another at least half a dozen times, concerns tobacco. Someone, usually Nobody – although the first time, it's Thel, and much later on, it's Benmont Tench (Jared Harris), a crazed trapper – asks William Blake if he has any tobacco, and Blake replies that he doesn't smoke. What makes this a gag is basically two interlocking ideas that inform one another. Firstly, contemporary American Puritanism – which treats smoking as something far worse than a health hazard to both the smoker and others, apparently because it affords pleasure to the smoker – is founded on a litany of denial that becomes enacted and re-enacted by this recurring exchange. It has also, by now, influenced or helped to impose various kinds of smoking restrictions in a good many places across the world. And, secondly, part of what's being denied is a social sacrament, especially among Native Americans.

ROSENBAUM: The funny thing about the tobacco joke is that, like so much in the movie, I took it as a commentary on America right now. Like the fact that Dickinson hires three bounty hunters to go after Blake and then sends other people out too. Kent Jones said to me that was like the way Hollywood studios hire screenwriters. (Dickinson even uses the word 'exclusive'!)

JARMUSCH (laughing): Good point – that's true. But to talk about tobacco, there were indigenous to North America some forty strains of tobacco that were far more powerful than anything we have now. I have a real respect for tobacco as a substance, and it just seems funny how the [non-Indian] Western attitude is, 'Wow, people are addicted to this, think of all the money you can make off of this.' For indigenous people here, it's still a sacrament; it's what you bring to someone's house, it's what you smoke when you pray. Our cultural adviser, Kathy [Whitman], is a member of the Native American Church and even uses peyote ceremonially. We used to go up on these hillsides sometimes early in the morning before shooting, usually with just the native people in the cast and crew, and pray and smoke. She'd put tobacco in a ceremonial pipe and pass it around, and you'd wash yourself with the smoke. She prays to each direction, to the sky, to the earth, to the plants and all the animals and animal spirits. And what cracked me up is, as soon as the ceremony was over, we'd be walking back down the hill and she'd be lighting up a Marlboro. She was very aware of the contradiction herself because I used to tease her about it.

Part of the comedy comes from the fact that Nobody's recurring question is a gesture of friendship that Blake can only read as something else, basically as a request for a handout. Indeed, it's characteristic of Blake

'Stupid fucking
white man'

throughout the film that even though he occasionally parrots the social or
poetic definitions imposed on him by others (turning into a cold-blooded
killer, as the wanted posters describe him, or even declaiming, 'Some are
born to endless night'), he never learns anything. He's as
uncomprehending about what's happening at the end of the film as he is at
the beginning. 'Stupid fucking white man,' another recurring phrase from
Nobody, couldn't describe him better. He's the ultimate butt of jokes by
Native Americans about their square and clueless oppressors, even when
they also happen to feel friendly towards them: 'Oh man, this white man
still doesn't get it.'

4 On Violence

I asked Jarmusch about the way he depicts violence.

ROSENBAUM: It seems like a key exchange when Blake asks Thel why she has a loaded pistol and she says, 'Cause this is America.' I believe you had a gun as a kid, didn't you?

JARMUSCH: I still have guns. And I'm not into killing living things, you know, but I'll always have guns. It seems so ingrained in America, but – well, the country was built on an attempted genocide, anyway. Guns were completely necessary. I find it very odd that the [US] amendment about the right to bear arms that the laws that were written so long ago still pertain and don't get adjusted properly. Because the right to bear arms doesn't mean automatic weaponry designed specifically for human combat. I think people should have the right to bear arms, but they should be limited as to what kinds of guns they can have.

The sudden deaths of Thel and Charlie Dickinson set the tone for Jarmusch's distinctive, unnerving handling of violence. Perhaps the film's most courageous defiance of commercial conventions is a response to the current cinema of violence that is so unsettling that audiences generally can't decide whether to wince or to laugh. Every time someone fires a gun at someone else in this film, the gesture is awkward, unheroic, pathetic; it's an act that leaves a mess and is deprived of any pretence at existential purity,

The awkwardness
of death

creating a sense of embarrassment and overall discomfort in the viewer that is the reverse of what ensues from the highly aestheticised forms of violence that have become *de rigueur* in commercial Hollywood ever since the heyday of Arthur Penn and Sam Peckinpah, and which have recently been revitalised by Tarantino, among others. In other words, Jarmusch refuses to respect or valorise bloodshed. And the film is no less honest about the allure of murderers in our culture; as Blake is gradually transformed into a cold-blooded killer, he takes on some of the 'legendary' aura of a media star.

For me, at least one part of the moral force of *Dead Man* is tied to this refusal of grace in relation to violence. But this isn't a refusal that carries over at all into *Ghost Dog*, where the violence is almost always graceful and the status of the title hero (Forest Whitaker) as a noble warrior is never questioned. Looking at the two films side by side and their almost opposite treatments of violence, I have to conclude that the moral force I associate with the awkward displays of violence in *Dead Man* isn't necessarily tied to Jarmusch's own conscious strategies – a clear instance of the intentional fallacy. I asked Jarmusch about this apparent discrepancy between the films, adding, 'Obviously the characters are different.'

JARMUSCH: You've just answered it completely. William Blake is an accountant. Even though he doesn't commit all the violence, this stuff is so foreign to him. He's pushed by circumstance into being an outlaw, completely against his own will. And Ghost Dog is a samurai; he studies the art of being a warrior, that is his obsession. The sword of a samurai is an extension of his soul, it's a physical extension of his spirit. Whereas Johnny's character doesn't know what the hell he's doing. He's surprised when the gun goes off. Also, the weapons are very different from what they are in *Ghost Dog*; they're much less precise. We did a lot of research into guns for *Dead Man* so as not to make any mistakes. I think the violence is much more stylised in *Ghost Dog*. In *Dead Man*, it's probably not that unrealistic, because boom! gun goes off and guys get hit with metal and fall down like puppets with strings getting cut – which is kind of what we wanted it to feel like, shocking for a brief moment and then very still. Someone's soul got taken.

'Looks like a goddamn religious icon'

One significant exception to the overall treatment of violence as graceless in *Dead Man* is a scene when Wilson happens upon the corpses of two marshals, he notes that the head of one of them 'looks like a goddamn religious icon' and promptly crushes it like a rotten cantaloupe under his heel – an image of astonishing, shocking beauty.

ROSENBAUM: Was that an homage to Sam Raimi?

JARMUSCH: Not specifically Sam Raimi, but I was aware of that genre of films, whether it be something from *The Evil Dead* or even Raúl Ruiz. I was definitely conscious that it was somewhat out of style in relation to my previous films, and maybe this film too, but I left it in. It's stylistically over the top, but it seems to fit with that guy's character. ... The cannibalism, too, is over the top.

How does one reconcile this moment with the depiction of violence elsewhere in the film? Basically one doesn't, although it might be said that

Forest Whitaker in
Ghost Dog

the gratuitous violence of white men plays a major part in this film, regardless of whether or not Jarmusch happens to treat it as graceful. The bottom line of both *Dead Man* and *Ghost Dog* is that violence is an omnipresent fact in American life and culture; how ugly or beautiful, meaningless or meaningful it happens to be in separate instances is mainly a matter of what tradition it aligns itself with – an issue of style as well as content.

5 On Music

In many ways, *Dead Man* has to be regarded as a distillation and fusion of a good many traditions, literary as well as cinematic, underground as well as mainstream, chemical as well as spiritual. Just as a term like 'acid Western', to be explored in Chapter 6, can't pretend to exhaust the film's drug-like handling of time and duration – opiates are clearly just as relevant to this project as hallucinogens – it would be misleading to suggest that literary and cinematic sources, explored in Chapter 7, comprise the sum of this movie's formal baggage. Jarmusch's brief stint as a musician around the same time as his first feature – he mainly played a 'fairly primitive Moog synthesizer' in a group called the Del Byzanteens – is probably as relevant to his subsequent film-making as his interest in poetry, and from its opening minutes, *Dead Man* reminds us constantly of this background.

Robby Müller's stunningly beautiful and exquisitely composed black-and-white cinematography, which includes a wide range of intermediate greys, is punctuated by fade-outs and black-outs between scenes, as if giving us forecasts of Blake's death even before he's wounded. Playing against the rhythms of the westbound train at the very beginning of the film, these interludes of unconsciousness or something resembling dream time create a form of suspension that continues periodically throughout the film, and are an essential part of Neil Young's haunting score, one of the greatest in contemporary movies.

ROSENBAUM: One thing I really like about *Dead Man* is that it's the one film of yours apart from *Stranger Than Paradise* that really establishes a rhythm all its own, one that's not the rhythm of any other film. It seems that part of this has to do with the fade-outs.

JARMUSCH: Yeah, I think you're right. But I'm the worst person to analyse the stuff and I hate looking back at it. I unfortunately had to look at *Stranger* again recently [in 1996] to prepare the laserdisc release in the States, which was really painful; I hadn't seen it since 1984. But I think there is something similar to them in that they do have very particular rhythms that seem to grow out of the stories themselves. It doesn't seem imposed in the same way that it might be in *Down by Law* or the more formally episodic ones. It does have a very odd rhythm. I think of it – and I don't know if this is accurate at all, it's just in my mind – as being closer to classical Japanese films rhythmically. We had that in the back of our minds while shooting, that scenes would resolve in and of themselves without being determined by the next incoming image.

ROSENBAUM: How long was the rough cut that Neil Young improvised his score to?

JARMUSCH: Two and a half hours. He refused to have the film stop at any moment. He did that three times over a two-day period. Neil asked me to give him a list of places where I wanted music, and he used that as a kind of map, but he was really focused on the film, so the score kind of became his emotional reaction to the movie. Then Neil came to New York to premix the stuff and we thought in a few places we'd slide it around a little, but it almost never worked – in general it was married to where he played it.

ROSENBAUM: Was your final editing influenced by what he did?

JARMUSCH: No, oddly enough. Or maybe it was, subconsciously. The final movie is two hours long and very little of Neil's music is missing, so we didn't cut much where there was music. But it wasn't a conscious decision.

Most of Young's minimalist score, recorded in a large warehouse in San Francisco, consists of electric guitar (with feedback) playing the same haunting and plaintive theme, with variations, over and over; the remainder is performed on acoustic guitar, pump organ and detuned piano and often registers as percussive sound effects, jolts of raw sensation. At times it calls to mind Jimi Hendrix's apocalyptic 'Star-Spangled Banner', but its most often repeated melodic phrase resembles, in both shape and feeling, 'Sometimes I Feel Like a Motherless Child', pointing to the absolute aloneness of both Blake and Nobody, together and separately, even as friends and companions.

As Jarmusch noted in an interview with Thomas Colbath and Stephen Blush, part of his model and inspiration for the pared-down score of *Dead Man* was the electric guitar music by Eric Clapton that was used in the 1984 British thriller *The Hit*. As Jarmusch recalled, Young's own conceptualisation for this partially improvised score was, "'To me, the movie is my rhythm section and I will add a melody to that,'" and he compared Young's method of performing live to a projection of the two-and-half-hour rough cut to the musical accompaniments of silent cinema,[17] though one could also cite the recording of certain improvised jazz scores in the 50s and 60s – most notably the improvisations done for Louis Malle's *Ascenseur pour l'échafaud* (*Frantic*, 1957) by Miles Davis, Barney Wilen, René Urtreger, Pierre Michelot and Kenny Clarke, and for John Cassavetes's *Shadows* (1960) by Charlie Mingus, Phineas Newborn Jr., and Shafi Hadi.[18] Like these precedents, Young's noodling and needling on the soundtrack function as a kind of impromptu Greek chorus, responding directly to various on-screen events and providing a laconic commentary.

Elsewhere in our conversation, Jarmusch elaborated that the film's odd, generally slow rhythm – hypnotic if you're captivated by it, as I am, and probably unendurable if you're not – was influenced by classical Japanese period movies by Mizoguchi and Kurosawa, and the tendency of scenes in those movies to exist in isolation from one another as complete units, like beads on a string. And the jangling, throbbing pulses of Young's music – the only unambiguously twentieth-century element in a nineteenth-century story – sometimes paradoxically recall the Japanese music and percussion used in some of those same films.

Young's brilliant album of 'music from and inspired by' *Dead Man*, lasting slightly over an hour, which often registers like an alternate version of the film – a composer's cut, as it were – reconfigures this relation between past and present by periodically including the sounds of cars passing on a highway. It also features not only patches of dialogue from the film, but also out-of-character readings by Johnny Depp of other Blake poems that were never part of the film, even on the script level.

Without picking up on the Japanese element, the first four of Greil

Marcus's 'Ten reasons why Neil Young's *Dead Man* is the best music for the dog days of the 20th century' point to comparable meditative qualities in this score:

1. For a film set more than a century ago, an electric guitar, playing a modal melody, surrounded by nothing, sounds older than anything you see on the screen.
2. The modal melody is never resolved, never completed. It feels less like a song than a fanfare, a fanfare for a parade no one ever got around to organizing.
3. The fanfare is stirring nevertheless. It's life and death from the start – or rather life staring death in the face. Death is going to win, but not even death knows how long it's going to take. Nobody, the Indian who tries and fails to dig a bullet out of Depp's William Blake … speaks of 'the white man who killed you'; 'I'm not dead,' Depp says. Nobody doesn't laugh. Young's guitar speaks for him, just as Nobody insists William Blake will now make his poetry with a gun.
4. Young doesn't laugh, either. His guitar doesn't even crack a smile.[19]

Jim Jarmusch and Neil Young

It's worth adding that Young was sufficiently happy about his collaboration with Jarmusch to invite him to make a concert documentary about his group Crazy Horse on tour the same year, which became Jarmusch's next film, *The Year of the Horse* (1997). It's an entertaining music documentary but not an especially ambitious work; I suspect that Jarmusch was somewhat hampered in having to incorporate footage already filmed by others during Crazy Horse's 1976 and 1986 tours.

Finally, it's worth noting that a number of anachronistic musical in-jokes can be traced through some of the characters' names and dialogue in *Dead Man*, creating even more allusions than the occasional film references. Among those cited by Jarmusch are 'Wilson Pickett' (which can be extracted from the surnames of two of the bounty hunters, Cole Wilson and Johnny 'The Kid' Pickett) and 'Lee Hazelwood' (the name of one of the two marshals shot by Blake – whose first name, as noted earlier, can also be combined with that of his partner, Marvin Throneberry, to yield 'Lee Marvin'). Moreover, Nobody's Indian nickname, 'He Who Talks Loud Saying Nothing', derives from James Brown's 'Talkin' Loud and Sayin' Nothing', and even the line 'My name is Nobody,' which some commentators have linked to the 1973 Italian Western produced by Sergio Leone, is for Jarmusch a reference to Conway Twitty.[20]

6 On the Acid Western

I

This is the Western Andrei Tarkovsky always wanted to make.
  J. Hoberman[21]

Although _Dead Man_ is obviously some kind of Western, it's not one of those smart homages to a Hollywood genre (like Sam Raimi's _The Quick and the Dead_) – it's more like the ghostly burnt-out shell of a Western, commandeered for sullen and obscure purposes.
  Adrian Martin[22]

JARMUSCH: I recently came across this interesting quote from Sam Peckinpah: 'The Western is a universal frame within which it's possible to comment on today.' Of course, I only saw this quote after I made _Dead Man_.

ROSENBAUM: I'm reminded of that Robert Aldrich Western of 1972, _Ulzana's Raid_, which a lot of people said at the time was really about the war in Vietnam.

JARMUSCH: In Hollywood Westerns, even in the 30s and 40s, history was mythologised to accommodate some kind of moral code. And what really affects me deeply is when you see it taken to the extent where Native Americans become mythical people. I think it's in _The Searchers_ where John Ford had some Indians who were supposedly Comanche, but he cast Navajos who spoke Navajo. It's kind of like saying, 'Yes, I know they are supposed to be French people, but I could only get Germans, and no one will know the difference.'

  It's really close to apartheid in America. The people in power will do whatever they can to maintain that, and TV and movies are perfect ways to keep people stupid and brainwashed. In regards to _Dead Man_, I just wanted to make an Indian character who wasn't either (a) the savage that must be eliminated, the force of nature that's blocking the way for industrial progress, or (b) the noble innocent that knows all and is another cliché. I wanted him to be a complicated human being.

ROSENBAUM: Right, but he's an outsider too, even to his own tribe. And given where we're at in terms of awareness of Native Americans, it somehow seems significant that in order to give him coherence, you have to route him through Europe.

JARMUSCH: I don't know. Like the slaughtering of buffalo, that was based on real accounts that I read. I read accounts of Natives that were taken all the way to Europe and put on display in London and Paris, and paraded like animals. ... I also read accounts of chiefs that were taken east and then murdered by their own tribes when they got back because of the stories they told about the white man – which became part of Nobody's story.

What was more fascinating to me is that these cultures coexisted only so briefly, and then the industrialised one eliminated the aboriginal culture. Those specific northwest tribes existed for thousands of years and then they were wiped out in much less than a hundred years. They even used biological warfare, giving them infected blankets and all kinds of stuff – any way to get rid of them. And then they were gone. And it was such an incredibly rich culture.

I don't really know of any fiction film where you see a Pacific northwest culture. I know there's the film *In the Land of the War Canoes*[23] made by Edward Curtis, the early twentieth-century photographer – he shot some Kwakiutl people, but it's sort of a *Nanook of the North* deal where he used them pretty much as actors. But their culture was so rich because where they lived provided them with salmon, and they could smoke that and exist all winter long without having to hunt very much. Therefore they spent a lot of time developing their architecture, their carving, their mythology and their incredibly elaborate ceremonies with these gigantic figures that would transform from one thing into another, with all kinds of optical illusions and tricks. That's why the longhouse opens that way in *Dead Man*, when Nobody goes inside to talk to the elders of the tribe and eventually gets a sea canoe from them. It seems to open magically, but it's based on a real system of pulleys that these tribes used.

In a masters thesis in anthropology written in 1998 for the University of British Columbia, Todd J. Tubutis notes that although the Makah settlement at the end of *Dead Man* is never verbally identified as such, great pains were taken to ensure its authenticity. Roughly three years after the filming, Tubutis interviewed eight Makah individuals who worked on the production – six as actors, two as set artists – and arrived at the following conclusions, among others:

In discussing historical sites, [Edward M. Bruner] delineated four meanings of 'authentic': verisimilitude, genuineness, originality, and authority. In creating the Makah village, Jarmusch operated with all four definitions in mind. First, he wanted the village to resemble an actual Northwest Coast village and he succeeded. Not only did Makah participants feel the village looked accurate, a friend remarked to me after seeing the film, 'How did Jarmusch get permission to film in the longhouse like that?' Second, he modeled the set on Ozette longhouses and old photographs so the set would appear genuine. Third, Jarmusch brought actual museum artifacts to decorate the set, hired Makah artists to construct artwork *in situ*, and asked for accurate Makah dialogue from the [Makah Cultural and Research Center], establishing a veneer of originality for the set. Fourth, he hired a First Nations Cultural Advisor to effectively 'certify' the set as appropriately 'Native': following cultural protocol equates to being authentic. [...]

   Future Makah audiences will be able to view *Dead Man* much as contemporary [Kwakiutl] audiences watch [*In the Land of the War Canoes*], looking for family, watching how the actors portrayed daily life, and admiring the work of artists on the set.[24]

II

In more ways than one *Dead Man* can be seen as the much-delayed fulfilment of a cherished counter-cultural dream which I'd like to call the acid Western. To varying degrees and in different respects, this generic ideal has haunted such films as Monte Hellman's *The Shooting* and *Ride the Whirlwind* (both 1967) and *Two-Lane Blacktop* (1971), Jim McBride's *Glen and Randa* and Dennis Hopper's *The Last Movie* (both 1971), Robert Downey's *Greaser's Palace* (1972), Alexander Jodorowsky's *El topo* (1972),

and – a much later example – Alex Cox's *Walker* (1987), not to mention
such novels as Rudolph Wurlitzer's *Nog* (1969) and *Flats* (1970) and Jim
Dodge's *Stone Junction* (1990). Wurlitzer, who worked on the scripts of
Glen and Randa, *Two-Lane Blacktop* and *Walker* – as well as Sam
Peckinpah's *Pat Garrett and Billy the Kid*; *Gone Beaver* (a visionary script of
the early 70s by Jim McBride and Lorenzo Mans, for a million-dollar
Western about trappers that never got filmed); and even a discarded early
draft of *Dead Man* – is surely the individual most responsible for exploring
this genre, having practically invented it himself in the late 60s and then
helped to nurture it in the scripts of others.

Greaser's Palace

Walker

What I partly mean by 'acid Westerns' are revisionist Westerns in which American history is reinterpreted to make room for peyote visions and related hallucinogenic experiences, LSD trips in particular. The influence of marijuana on the drifting, nonlinear aspects of the style of *McCabe and Mrs. Miller*, which seems partially reflected in the importance of opium in the plot, is related but still somewhat distinct from the paradigm I have in mind, by virtue of being less radical an upheaval of generic norms. Both 'acid Westerns' and 'pot Westerns' depend on re-evaluations of white and nonwhite experience that view certain counter-cultural habits and styles in relation to models derived from Westerns, but where they differ most, perhaps, is in their generational biases, which lead them respectively to overturn or ironically revise the relevant generic norms.

ROSENBAUM: Part of what I'm calling 'acid Westerns' and you've sometimes called 'peripheral Westerns' has to do with certain literary ideas about the wilderness and travelling from the east coast to the west coast. In most Western versions of the east-to-west journey, there's a movement towards enlightenment and freedom, but *Dead Man* almost reverses that, turning the story into a movement towards death. And if you think of all the white people that Blake and Nobody run into, they all seem to fit into two categories some version of capitalism or some version of the counter-culture, sometimes the two mixed together.

JARMUSCH: Yeah, they coexist somehow. And the counter-culture is always repackaged and made into a product, y'know? It's part of America. If you have a counter-culture and you put a name on it, you call them beatniks, and you can sell something – books or bebop. Or you label them as hippies and you can sell tie-dyed T-shirts.

ROSENBAUM: But then there's also Iggy Pop in that dress. What's disturbing about *Dead Man* is that the whole sense of society – which is always pretty attenuated in your films to begin with – is pretty nightmarish whenever it turns up. You get the feeling that between these isolated outposts of civilisation, anything can happen. You can't always distinguish between what's real and what's inside your head.

JARMUSCH: Yeah. And I think when Blake encounters the trappers, it's like here is a trace element of the family unit that has gotten so perverted out here, because these guys live out in the fuckin' nowhere. Yet there's some slight thread of a family unit that they've adapted between themselves – which is absurd on one level, but on another level it's exactly what you're saying. They're way out there. I don't know if you can hear it, but when Iggy's trying to load up his shotgun, he's complaining, 'I cooked, I cleaned ...'

I don't agree with a colleague of mine who calls this scene homophobic; in this sort of context, gender is but a glancing detail in an overall context of multifaceted backwoods contrariness. But there's no question that it's playing with all sorts of excess in terms of its gallows humour and is as hyperbolic in a way as the head-crushing scene, simultaneously hilarious and terrifying. The demented trio of 'Sally' Jenko (Iggy Pop), Big George Drakoulious (Billy Bob Thornton) and Benmont Tench (Jared Harris) are clearly designed to suggest redneck trappers from hell, as obsessed with the Good Book as they are with the texture of Blake's hair. ('By God it *is* soft. Now how do you get it that way? See, this old stuff-a mine is like old barn hay, there ain't a dern thing you can do with it.') The whole scene has the feel of actors improvising in a free-wheeling 'Can you top this?' spirit. (There's even a reprise of the recurring tobacco gag.) I don't know whether it was literally improvised, in whole or in part, but the script Jarmusch gave me sketches in only the barest rudiments of the action apart from the deaths of all three characters at the end, with all the dialogue 'to be determined'. Much of it seems sculpted around the proclivities of the actors: e.g. after Benmont and Big George start fighting over Blake ('This one's mine, Big George! You had the last one!') and the former shoots the latter in the foot – shortly before Nobody steps forward and, literally accompanied by a bolt of lightning, slits Big George's throat – Big George delivers a kind of short verbal cadenza that would have been fairly pointless without Thornton's southern accent: 'Good God, I'm hit! Lord have mercy – burns like hellfire – son of a bitch. I'm gonna have to kill somebody now.'

The fact that the scene opens with 'Sally' reading aloud to the others from 'Goldilocks and the Three Bears' (followed by the Bible, along with helpful definitions of words like 'scourge' and 'philistine', after she serves beans) suggests that here and occasionally elsewhere in *Dead Man*, Jarmusch is using the Western form to spin something of a fairy tale himself, with the trio here figuring as sinister fairy-tale villains – discovering an imaginative freedom through his speculative look at the past that would have been relatively unthinkable in his earlier films (even if he did briefly give us the ghost of Elvis in *Mystery Train*).

III

These are *Dead Man*'s final lines of dialogue:

NOBODY
I prepared your canoe with cedar bows. It's time for you to leave now, William Blake. Time for you to go back to where you came from.

BLAKE
You mean Cleveland?

NOBODY
Back to the place where all the spirits come from, and where all the spirits return. This world will no longer concern you.

BLAKE
(*holding up a twist of tobacco*)
I found some tobacco.

NOBODY
The tobacco is for your voyage, William Blake.
NOBODY *pushes off* BLAKE's *sea canoe*.

BLAKE
Nobody – I don't smoke.

'Forms have disintegrated here [on the East Coast] so you're involved in disintegration,' Wurlitzer noted in an interview roughly three decades ago. 'But out there [on the West Coast] forms just *aren't* there. In that sense it's a weird frontier, where you don't have to be historically located … .[It's] much easier to become freer from your conditioning. No, let's say it's easier not to have conditioning.'[25]

Although this doesn't literally replicate the evolution of William Blake's journey from Cleveland – Jarmusch's home town – towards his own death, it does at least correspond to a certain cleansing away of history and civilisation as he moves from Machine towards the west coast. 'History' and 'civilisation' in this context actually mean genocide, the Industrial Revolution and the concomitant destruction of nature, the spread of capitalism and the concomitant destruction of barter systems, and even the spread of Christianity. (The latter is shockingly associated in *Dead Man* with both the psychosis and violence of the 'family' of trappers and the hypocrisy and racism of the missionary at the trading post, who prompts Nobody to quote what may well be his most apposite citation from Blake: 'The Vision of Christ that thou dost see/Is my Vision's Greatest Enemy.')

An important part of what I've been calling the acid Western involves the replacement of capitalism with alternative models of social exchange proposed by the counter-culture that took root during the 60s. In the novels and scripts of Wurlitzer, a practising Buddhist for the past quarter of a century, this has often involved the deliberate relinquishing of power, which represents the closest thing in his work to utopia.[26] In the comics of a counter-cultural artist like Robert Crumb, it entails a mistrust of institutions, a mockery of certain contemporary fashions and a nostalgia for certain older forms of American pop culture. And in Jarmusch's own work, this has involved a *nostalgie de la boue* – a stylistic, existential and bohemian embrace of downscale modes of living. All these attitudes can be found to some degree in *Dead Man*, and this is far from being an exhaustive list. It demonstrates that certain political allegiances play a much more important role in such alignments than particular generations, because Jarmusch is about ten years younger than Crumb and sixteen years younger than Wurlitzer – making him only seven years old when the 60s began.

Just as the 40s, 50s and 60s of the just-completed century were largely informed by the political divisions that took shape in society in relation to the ferment and challenges of the 30s, one might argue that the 70s, 80s and 90s were no less affected by the divisions formed in relation to the 60s. From this standpoint, *Dead Man* may have even more to do with the 60s than it does with either the decade in which it's set or the decade in which it was made. (Perhaps to the same degree, the more recent *American Beauty* [1999] offers a quintessential expression of the values of the 70s.)

IV

Gregg Rickman proposes at least three other kinds of Western *Dead Man* can be regarded as – comic Western, ironic Western and 'Western under erasure'. Supporting the first model is the fact that 'Bill Blake is a protagonist who never learns anything from his ordeal. He is a traveler across a mythic landscape who remains oblivious to it' – a 'Dead Man Wearing Plaid', as Rickman's witty section heading puts it, or 'absurdist' hero who belongs in the company of Douglas Fairbanks in *Wild and Wooly* (1917), Buster Keaton in several 20s features, James Stewart in *Destry Rides Again* (1939) and Bob Hope in *The Paleface* (1948).

Yet 'Blake's extraordinary passivity' for Rickman ultimately distinguishes him from 'the comic hero of classical Westerns', so he turns next to the model of 'ironic Western' citing in particular the 1973 Italian Western and Sergio Leone parody appropriately titled *My Name is Nobody*, and proposing that Nobody may in fact be the true protagonist of *Dead Man*, '[using] Blake as a means of re-entering Native American culture, selling his vision of Blake as a spiritual heir of William Blake to the Makah community of the Pacific Northwest, and winning approval to use a sea canoe for the dying Blake'. Certainly the degree to which Nobody's utter isolation, as suggested by his very name, goes beyond that of Blake, raises the possibility that the poetry of solitude considered so basic to the Western as a genre – forming the essence of every Western hero from Shane and Ethan Edwards to John McCabe to Clint Eastwood's various lone figures – applies more in this case to the Indian than to the cowboy, further suggesting that Jarmusch may be revitalising the essentials of the form in spite of himself.

But the absurdist means by which Nobody and Cole Wilson kill one another during the closing minutes of *Dead Man* (which I'll discuss again later) eventually lead Rickman to a third and more confident model, the 'Western under erasure' in which everything is 'ultimately ... canceled by something else', making *Dead Man* 'a nihilist statement of protest' that offers 'no viable positive alternative to Machine civilization'.[27]

The term 'under erasure', derived from Martin Heidegger by way of Jacques Derrida, is used to describe a form of self-cancelling writing, the strategy of using the only language that one has at one's disposal without subscribing to its premises, yielding certain words that are crossed out but can still be read. As Gayatri Chakravorty Spivak puts it parenthetically in her Preface to Derrida's *Of Grammatology*, 'Since the word is inaccurate, it is crossed out. Since it is necessary, it remains legible.'[28]

Back in the early 80s, J. Hoberman and I applied this terminology, after a bit of boiling and scraping, to David Lynch's *Eraserhead,* mainly as a way of accounting for Lynch's ambivalent self-censoring Puritanism – a conflict present in the film's very title whose gestural equivalent would be placing one's hands over one's eyes and then peeking through them.[29] Rickman uses the terminology somewhat differently: proposing that Blake may already be dead before the action of *Dead Man* begins and that he may be 'trapped in some sort of time loop', Rickman compares him to the character Fred Madison in Lynch's *Lost Highway*.[30] It's a tempting hypothesis given the circularity implied by the opening monologue of the train's fireman, but I'm not at all sure that Jarmusch's brooding imagination and dark humour belong in the same universe as Lynch's. Indeed, the moment one tries to situate these two film-makers historically, ideologically and even morally, they immediately break off into opposing camps, Lynch becoming aligned with the conservative side of the 50s as fully as Jarmusch is associated with the rebel forces of the subsequent two decades. Consequently, I resist any analytical grid that would imply some sort of equivalence between the lurid disavowals of Lynch and the generic subversions of Jarmusch.

To my mind, Jarmusch's somewhat disrespectful treatment of the Western as a genre is a function of several intertwining impulses, including an inclination towards epic or lyric poetry and away from prose narrative, a distaste for the usual white myths about Indians, and an impatience with certain Western conventions such as The Final Shootout that encourages him to use them derisively. In the latter instance, one might argue that another attempt to subvert The Final Shootout in a different manner at the end of *Ghost Dog* produces results that are no less unsatisfying. In *Dead Man*, the jarringly comic way in which both Nobody and Cole Wilson appear to drop dead simultaneously after spinning in semi-circles, in extreme long shot, is in striking contrast to the gravity with which Blake's own impending death is treated. Maybe the problem can be traced back to a conceptual impasse arising from the equivalent of a mixed metaphor: the 'single metaphor that the physical life is this journey that we take' cited by Jarmusch becomes less simple if Nobody and Wilson have to be accorded narrative closure along with Blake, so maybe they both get killed simply because Jarmusch doesn't know what else to do with them at this juncture. (As a sort of stepson of the French New Wave, Jarmusch may have even been guided by the frequent practice of ending New Wave features with the gratuitous deaths of leading characters.) And not wanting to steal any thunder from the death of Blake, the film's ruling metaphor, Jarmusch can only make these relatively sudden and unheralded deaths occur like a simple pirouette.

What's especially off-putting about this moment is that Gary Farmer's Nobody is conceivably the richest and most nuanced performance to be found in any Jarmusch film – making him the most fully realised character in Jarmusch's work – yet he's killed off at the end as if he were a minor character, almost as a kind of afterthought. (Could this partially account for why Jarmusch resurrects the character in *Ghost Dog* – to give him a more proper burial?) Even if one takes into account the mythological overdeterminations that make Nobody a questionable creation for some viewers – one, in particular, has complained to me that the usual mutual alienation between Plains Indians and Indians of the northwest coast would have made it unlikely that Nobody would have been able to either speak Makah or to procure a sea canoe for Blake at the Makah settlement – the density and humanity of his embodiment by

Farmer put him in a very special category. (By contrast, Johnny Depp's superbly iconic rendering of Blake gains much of its luminosity and gravity from his allegorical resonance.) Surely the fact that Nobody would have learned Blake's poetry as a boy in England is no less of a stretch than the possibility that he might have learned Makah as an adult during his wanderings in the US as an outcast. Indeed, his isolation from most white and Indian people alike makes these two forms of specialised knowledge rather complementary. (One might add that his pariah status in relation to both Blood and Blackfoot Indians is a key indication in *Dead Man* that intolerance isn't merely the invention of whites but a universal disease, and an indication that Jarmusch isn't following the p.c. prescription of depicting Native Americans who are without prejudice.)

It's a somewhat unnerving last-minute shift in tone, but not a fatal one – because the literal way in which Nobody and Wilson cancel each other out as narrative strands allows the film to end with Blake alone, which is more or less how it began. Paradoxically, then, *Dead Man* ends with a variation of the archetypal last shot of the classic Western – the lone hero receding into the distance. He may be sailing off in a boat rather than

Sailing into oblivion

riding away on horseback like Shane (the camera took sympathetic leave of Blake's own stranded and confused horse at the trading post, when Blake and Nobody boarded their first canoe), and he may be bound for oblivion rather than another adventure, but the epic sense of closure is satisfyingly complete. It literally duplicates the graphic form of the opening credits, each successive title receding frontally from the foreground into the distance – except for the title *Dead Man* itself, lettered in assemblies of bones that disperse and then dissolve after they retreat.

The opening titles

　　Part of the satisfaction to be found in the Western genre is the recurrence of a recognisable and elaborately furnished universe. *Dead Man* alludes to that universe at every turn without ever completely conforming to it; a revisionist impulse insists on rethinking virtually all the basic props and images associated with the form, much (if not all) of which comprises a kind of ongoing historical critique. On the train, for instance, Blake's fancy duds, cravat and all, are more than faintly comic (Rickman's allusion to Bob Hope in *The Paleface* is especially relevant here), but few if any of the costumes worn by extras qualify as standard-issue for Westerns. The initial sights that Blake glimpses fearfully on the main street of Machine are comparably off-kilter in terms of our general expectations (how many Western main streets feature pissing horses or blowjobs?); the Dickinson industrial plant registers like a nightmare out of Dickens, and even the miniature bottle of whiskey that Blake subsequently purchases in a saloon comes across as slightly unsettling. In similar fashion, one could run through the remainder of the film ticking

Bob Hope in *The Paleface*

off various ways, both large and small, in which the sense of detail dislodges generic norms. Not all of Jarmusch's subversions necessarily conform to a more realistic historical model of the Western. Some – such as the bolt of lightning just before Nobody slits the throat of Big George

Jolting realism

Drakoulious, or the accidental way in which his rifle goes off and kills 'Sally' Jenko just afterwards – are more like pure flights of fancy. But virtually all of them follow a consistent pattern of combining traditional elements with transgressive details, almost as if Jarmusch wanted to give us a version of the classic Western reconfigured as some sort of nightmare.

Blake's delirious impressions of the Makah village, fading in and out of legibility and consciousness, perfectly illustrate the film's overall strategy of 'making strange': on the one hand, a simple itinerary of prosaic and everyday sights and events, rendered almost anthropologically; on the other hand, a series of slow lap dissolves that merge and confuse these simple perceptions. This sequence forms a precise inversion of the equally subjective and no less disorienting glimpses of various grim events on Machine's main street, where the style is relatively straightforward and the content is considerably more grotesque. It's also a contrast between

Blake's delirium

capitalism and barter, between industrial and pre-industrial societies, and the fact that Blake experiences some fear and confusion in relation to both communities epitomises the sort of social alienation he shares with Nobody. By the time they reach this coastal settlement, they've clearly reached the end as far as America and its possibilities are concerned, making the deaths of both characters in this location seem inevitable.

7 Frontier Poetry

I

ROSENBAUM: In a recent essay about the dumbing down of American movies, Phillip Lopate writes, 'Take Jim Jarmusch: a very gifted, intelligent filmmaker, who studied poetry at Columbia, yet he makes movie after movie about low-lifes who get smashed every night, make pilgrimages to Memphis where they are visited by Elvis's ghost, shoot off guns and in general comport themselves in a somnambulistic, inarticulate, unconscious manner.'[31]

JARMUSCH: I don't know, man. Once I was in a working-class restaurant in Rome with Roberto [Begnini] at lunchtime. They had long tables where you sit with other people. We sat down with these people in their blue work overalls, they were working in the street outside, and Roberto's talking to them, and they started talking about Dante and Ariosto and twentieth-century Italian poets. Now you go out to fucking Wyoming and go in a bar and mention the word 'poetry', and you get a gun stuck up your ass. That's the way America is. Whereas even guys who work in the street collecting garbage in Paris love nineteenth-century painting. I don't know, am I supposed to put on a false voice and say, 'Here are the rare exceptions, and we should be like them?' There's a subculture now that even roads, that's really cool, but they are not in any sense any kind of majority; that's not normal American life…. And you know, if the media notices it, it isn't a subculture any more.

One possible reason why there's seldom been much agreement about what constitutes a literary film is a common bias against film as an art form within the literary world, especially the Anglo-American branches of it. It's a bias inflected with a sense of unfair competition or outright usurpment, whether this comes from English professors resenting the popularity of movies with their students or from novelists who have seen favourite works (including some of their own) diluted and vulgarised by film adaptations. The degree to which these adaptations often serve as some viewers' reductive substitutes for the original books – thereby accounting for some of the dubious popularity and prestige of Jane Austen and Henry James adaptations in recent years, their capacity to make some viewers feel 'well-read' without actually reading – makes this bias somewhat understandable. But at the same time it often regrettably rules out the very possibility of other kinds of literary films – films informed and enhanced by literary qualities that are original works rather than adaptations. (The relative ease with which a Marguerite Duras or an Alain Robbe-Grillet can shift from novels to films and back again suggests that within French culture it's easier to think of film-making as 'literature by other means'.)

To my mind, *Dead Man* is just such a film, straddling the realms of literature and cinema with ease, though one reason why it isn't widely recognised as such is the habit of viewing films as fictional narratives and not as poems – that is, as vehicles for stories rather than words. Yet as literary critic William Troy once noted, 'A word, in the terminology of modern physics, is a time-space event,'[32] which theoretically suggests that the realms of literature and cinema are not quite as incompatible as some commentators pretend. Certainly literature takes on an importance in *Dead Man* that it has not previously had in Jarmusch's work, and in certain significant respects *Ghost Dog* sustains it – not only through the many quotations from the book mentioned in the subtitle, and the central functioning of that book in the life of its title hero, but also through the circulation of and discussions about Mary Shelley's *Frankenstein* and Ryunosuke Akutagawa's *Rashomon*.

Although Jarmusch is personally a very skilful raconteur, it might be argued that his talent as a comic performer has more to do with a flair for mimicking various voices and accents than with an ability to recount long stories, at least in any detail. The nuts and bolts of extended narrative are not generally his forte, which may help to explain why he characteristically glides past such matters as the logistics of how the three heroes of *Down by Law* escape from prison or precisely how various bounty hunters and marshals follow the trail of William Blake in *Dead Man*. It probably isn't accidental that Jarmusch's features tend to be episodic – either extended narratives broken up into 'chapters' such as *Stranger Than Paradise* and

Down by Law or collections of separate (if temporally overlapping) short stories in *Mystery Train* and *Night on Earth*.

As noted earlier, Jarmusch studied poetry as an undergraduate at Columbia University, and reportedly contemplated becoming a poet before he travelled to Paris, attended screenings at the Cinémathèque Française, and, after his return to the States, wound up joining New York University's graduate programme in film production (where he made *Permanent Vacation* as his thesis film – although it wasn't accepted as such by the faculty, apparently for technical reasons, and he didn't receive a degree until much later, when he was offered an honorary degree). It wouldn't be unreasonable to claim that poetry has influenced his work more than prose fiction, but one problem with dealing with such an association is that film critics commonly confuse a generalised 'poetic sensibility' with the concrete form and practice of poetry. I've been guilty of this myself in such articles as 'The Problem with Poetry: Léos Carax',[33] influenced no doubt by the impressionism of a certain kind of French criticism, and much as Phillip Lopate has justifiably chided me and others for confusing the loosely-defined 'essayistic' impulse with the essay form,[34] it may be argued that many critics confuse 'poetic' with poetry to an equivalent degree. Kent Jones briefly touched on this problem in his review of *Dead Man*:

In film criticism and café conversation, the word 'poetic' generally applies to films that evoke a lofty *feeling* of 'poetry' (*Wings of Desire*, *The Piano*). *Dead Man* is actually structured as an epic film poem with rhyming figures (Blake's walk to the factory in Machine 'rhymes' with his final walk to the hut in the Indian village) and refrains (the film is punctuated by twisting journeys on horseback through rocky terrain, quotations from *the* William Blake, and the crashing tremors of Neil Young's feedback electric guitar score). Jarmusch also employs the rapid fades to black started during the train journey throughout the film. Sequences have no standardized shape, and the blackouts create an effect of pockets of time cupped from a rushing river of life.[35]

Interestingly, Jones's evocations of poetry gradually merge with evocations of music (e.g. 'refrains', the Neil Young score), and when we get to the

Nobody remembers

black-outs – or the white-outs during Nobody's flashbacks about his
boyhood – we could be speaking about either poetry or music: as in
Stranger Than Paradise, where the patches of black leader suggest both the
blank spaces on a page between stanzas and the pauses or rests between
musical statements, we have entered a realm where the two forms become
somewhat coterminous. In fact, these punctuations in *Stranger*, by
separating entire sequences, give the one-take sequences themselves a
sense of laconic completeness that calls to mind individual blues choruses
(and the blues, appropriately, comprises one of the forms in which poetry
and music meet).

The noblest antecedents of *Dead Man* as a disquieting apocalyptic
portrait are literary rather than cinematic. Consider William Blake's poem
'London':

I wander thro' each charter'd street,
Near where the charter'd Thames does flow,
And mark in every face I meet
Marks of weakness, marks of woe.

In every cry of every Man,
In every Infant's cry of fear,
In every voice, in every ban,
The mind-forg'd manacles I hear.

How the Chimney-sweeper's cry
Every black'ning Church appalls;
And the hapless Soldier's sigh
Runs in blood down Palace walls.

But most thro' midnight streets I hear
How the youthful Harlot's curse
Blasts the new born Infant's tear,
And blights with plagues the Marriage hearse.

And consider this from William S. Burroughs's *Naked Lunch*: 'America is not a young land: it is old and dirty and evil before the settlers, before the Indians. The evil is there waiting.'

These passages, written a little over a century and a half apart, describe worlds in which evil and blight are metaphysical principles – the contemporary world for Blake, and a seemingly timeless one for Burroughs. In a way, *Dead Man* grows out of a horrified view of industrialised America compatible with the apocalyptic visions of both Blake and Burroughs, superimposed over an image of the American west haunted by the massive slaughter of Native Americans. And because it contradicts or confounds much of our mythology about the Western – reversing some of its philosophical presuppositions by associating a westward journey with death rather than rebirth, for example, and with pessimism rather than hope – it shouldn't be too surprising that a fair number of Americans weren't ready for it in 1996. *Dead Man* implicitly rejects many of the recent staples of commercial film-making – the feel-good slaughterfests of Woo and Tarantino, the affectless formalism and callow merchandising of MTV, the plot-driven buddy movie – and chooses instead to meditate on the relation of death to the natural world. One key occurrence in the movie is the eerie, poetic, mystical moment when Blake, lost and alone in the wilderness, curls up alongside an accidentally slain fawn, after mixing some of its spilt blood with his own and smearing the blend on his face as a kind of impromptu war paint. (It's one of the most beautiful and mysterious scenes in the film and, according to Jarmusch, Depp improvised the face-painting.)

Much of the latter remains on Blake's face for the rest of the film, just as the identity of the poet William Blake eventually merges with his own – most clearly when he asks the marshals, 'Do you know my poetry?' before killing them. According to the film's alchemy whereby the poetry of Blake becomes a form of Native American wisdom, an accountant named Blake becomes both the poet and a Native American. Indeed, in this respect, Blake might be regarded throughout the film as a kind of mystic writing pad bearing the traces of other signatures.

ROSENBAUM: It's interesting how Blake picks up bits and pieces of his identity from other people in the film, including Nobody.

JARMUSCH: Yeah. He's also like a blank piece of paper that everyone wants to write all over, which is why I like Johnny [Depp] so much as the actor for that character, because he has that quality. He's branded an outlaw

Afternoon with a fawn

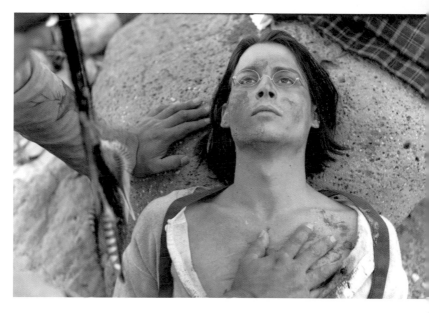

The face as writing pad

totally against his character, and he's told he's this great poet, and he doesn't even know what this crazy Indian is talking about. Even the scene in the trading post where the missionary [Alfred Molina] says, 'Can I have your autograph?' and then pulls a gun on him – and Blake stabs him in the hand and says, 'There, that's my autograph.' It's like all these things are projected onto him. When Nobody leaves him alone after taking peyote, Blake is left to go on his own vision quest briefly, whether he knows it or not, because he's fasting – not because he wants to but because he doesn't know how to eat out there. That's a really important ceremony of most North American tribes – a vision quest where you're left to fast, usually for a three-day period.

II

Here's a scene from the original script of *Dead Man* that doesn't appear in the final release version of the film, apart from a variation on Nobody's opening line of dialogue. This scene was positioned to occur just after

Dickinson dispatches the three bounty hunters ('Boys, the hunt is on') and would have been the second scene between Blake and Nobody if it had been included:

16. EXT. FOREST – LATE AFTERNOON
BLAKE's *eyes, in* CLOSE-UP. *Slowly they open –* BLAKE *returning to consciousness. He struggles to focus his vision, then sees the big* INDIAN *by the nearby fire, preparing more medicine and some food. The* INDIAN *notices that he is awake and glares over at him.*

> NOBODY
> Go back to sleep, stupid white man.

BLAKE *closes his eyes, but opens them again, wincing in pain. He touches his wound, then winces again, quickly pulling his hand away. He looks at the blood on his fingers. The* INDIAN *sees this and yells at* BLAKE *loudly.*

> NOBODY
> Stupid white man! Don't touch that!

He glares at BLAKE, *who draws a deep breath, exhaling slowly.*

> BLAKE
> (*after a pause*)
> Am ... I gonna die?

The INDIAN *looks at him for a long time, his expression itself revealing very little, but the hardness that was previously in his eyes has changed, softening somehow.*

> NOBODY
> The patterns in the clouds will answer this question.

His eyes then move away, returning to his preparations on the fire. Heavily, BLAKE *looks up into the pitch-black sky, then back down at the Indian, as though dreaming.*

> BLAKE
> (*after a long pause*)
> Why ... why are you helping me?

> NOBODY
> (*not looking up*)
> A bird told me.

BLAKE

What? [*pause*] A *bird* told you?

NOBODY

(*looking over, as though bored by the question*)

A small bird with very bright blue feathers. I was following him in the forest hoping to acquire one of his indigo feathers. And then I lost him. And then I found him again, and he was sitting on your chest, tasting your blood. And then he looked at me, and then flew directly west, in a very straight line, his small beak red with your blood.

The INDIAN *returns to his work.*

BLAKE

(*drowsily*)

A small ... bright blue bird ... tasted my blood ... [*then, as though surfacing unconsciously from a deep place in his memory*] 'Billy, the small blue birds are back ... they're in the mulberry tree ... the indigo buntings. ...'

He closes his eyes for a moment, then opens them halfway. The INDIAN's *eyes register surprise, and he studies* BLAKE *carefully, his interest piqued by something he has just said.*

NOBODY

How is it that you know the name of this magical bird, the indigo bunting?

BLAKE *offers no response, as though unaware of what he has said. His eyelids flutter a little.*

BLAKE

Are you a ... medicine man? [pause] And, how come you ... you speak such perfect English?

For some reason this angers the INDIAN, *and he glares and yells at* BLAKE.

NOBODY

Why is there metal in the stupid white man's heart?

BLAKE

(*at first confused*)

Metal in. ... Oh. I got. ... A man shot me. [*pause*] And he
killed Thel. ... He killed a ... beautiful woman. [*pause*] And
then I ... I killed him. [*pause*] I think I did anyway.

NOBODY
(*looking at him intensely*)
Was she your woman?

BLAKE
(*fingering the white paper rose in his lapel*)
I ... I, uh, ... I don't know, exactly.

This response angers the INDIAN *even more.*

NOBODY
Stupid fucking white man!

*Again he grabs a stick and breaks it in two, then stands and throws the pieces off
into the forest. He turns back to face* BLAKE, *looking down on him
threateningly, his eyes wild.*

NOBODY
(*sternly*)
All wholesome food is caught without a net or a trap!

He then turns and begins to pace around and around in a circle. BLAKE *watches
the* INDIAN's *consistent and dizzying movements. In* CLOSE-UP BLAKE's
*eyelids become heavy, as though hypnotised, then slowly close as he falls into
unconsciousness.*

ROSENBAUM: That's a very puzzling scene in the original script, when Blake asks
    Nobody, 'Why are you helping me?' and Nobody says, 'A bird told me.'
JARMUSCH: Oh yeah. I shot that, actually. The indigo bunting is a very
    psychedelic, bright, iridescent blue bird which is pretty small and very
    rare.
ROSENBAUM: Was that scene cut for length or some other reason?
JARMUSCH: It was cut for length. Things expand when you shoot them, and
    the first version of the film which had that scene was three hours long.
ROSENBAUM: I find the whole dialogue pretty strange and mysterious.
JARMUSCH: It was important to me because native or aboriginal cultures
    almost always consider animals to be spirit guides. In fact, I have a friend

who lives up in the country, he's a farmer now, and he lost a baby calf in the winter and couldn't find it. He spent all night looking, slept two hours, got up the next day at the crack of dawn, and this crow kept flying to him and flying off in the same direction, so he followed it, found the calf almost dead, lying behind some hay, and it was revived and saved. And then he told his neighbours, all these old farmer guys, 'I don't know if I'm smoking too much weed or what, but I swear this crow ...' and they said, 'No, crows will lead other animals out of forest fires – crows do that kind of shit.'

III

Dead Man proposes a cluster of metaphors: life as a journey (Blake's journey unwittingly becomes a spiritual quest), white man as dead man, Blake as death itself (such as when Nobody, on peyote, sees him turn into a skeleton), and poetry as something that white America is but doesn't know and can't understand. (A similar point was at least implied by Roberto Begnini's character in *Down by Law* – at least in relation to the comprehension of his American cellmates, played by John Lurie and Tom Waits.) Some of the Blake adages Nobody quotes – such as 'The eagle never lost so much time as when he submitted to learn of the crow' and 'Drive your cart and your plow over the bones of the dead,' both from *Proverbs of Hell* – sound like Native American sayings to Blake and to us, and conversely some of Nobody's own pronouncements sound like the poetry of Blake. As Jarmusch suggests above, Depp's luminous Blake, the

Nobody's peyote vision

central white man, is a blank sheet of paper that others – Dickinson, Nobody, the bounty hunters, the trio of trappers, the marshals, the racist missionary at the trading post and even the original William Blake – cover with their manic scribbles. Finally their preoccupations about him become both his identity and his fatal destiny: his renegade badge of honour, 'Some are Born to Endless Night', is taken from his namesake's *Auguries of Innocence*.

JARMUSCH: Blake just walked into the script right before I was starting to write it, up in the woods. He was sort of a late development because I was reading a lot of books by Indians, and to take a break from that, I just picked up a copy of the collected works of Blake there and started reading *Proverbs of Hell*. And that's when I thought, 'Wow, man, this is so close to the other stuff I've been reading.' You know – 'Expect poison from the standing water.' All those little aphorisms.

There were a bunch of other quotes like that that didn't get into the film that seemed very Native American: 'What is now proved was once only imagin'd.' 'The crow wish'd every thing was black, the owl that every thing was white.' And Nobody quotes from *The Everlasting Gospel* when they're at the trading post: 'The Vision of Christ that thou dost see/Is my Vision's Greatest Enemy.'

Intentionality is often an ungraspable and therefore somewhat bogus issue in criticism – if only because works (including words, sounds and images) invariably take on meanings independently of their authors and because conscious and unconscious motives are often impossible to sort out. Still, it might be instructive to note a few of the things that Jarmusch, by his own testimony, *didn't* have in mind when he scripted *Dead Man*. Given that the character of Thel clearly derives from *The Book of Thel*, a fact confirmed by Jarmusch, it might seem obvious to some readers that Nobody's name was suggested by Nobodaddy – a Blakean figure identified by Northrop Frye as 'the ill-tempered old man in the sky that results from our efforts to visualize a First Cause'.[36] But Jarmusch assured me that he was unaware of Nobodaddy, and that no such thought ever crossed his mind. He also volunteered that although he had read Homer's *Odyssey*, he had forgotten when he scripted *Dead Man* that in Book IX, Odysseus introduces himself to the Cyclops as Nobody; maybe this was an unconscious influence, but if so, the possibility hadn't occurred to him until he reread the passage. (As for cinematic influence, when I brought up the final shots of F. W. Murnau's *Tabu* [1931] in reference to *Dead Man*'s ending, he replied that he had seen it a long time ago and had been deeply moved by it, but it hadn't served as a conscious reference point.) On the other hand, Jarmusch pointed out to me that the name of John Hurt's character, John Scholfield, comes from the name of the dragoon who entered Blake's garden, quarrelled with him, and accused him of insulting the king, which led to a warrant being issued for Blake's arrest on the charge of sedition.

Yet as the point about Nobodaddy makes clear, it shouldn't be assumed that Jarmusch's use of Blake's poetry in *Dead Man* is informed by any consistent sort of literary scholarship. Jarmusch has noted in interviews that, although the film doesn't bother to mention it, *Dead Man* is set in the 1870s. Gregg Rickman has pointed out that the aforementioned *Auguries of Innocence*, though written in the early nineteenth century, wasn't published during Blake's lifetime, and came to light only in 1866, which means that 'Nobody would have to be markedly well placed to have read [the poem] during his sojourn in England, datable to the 1850s.'[37] But this is only to say that, like most literary works of distinction, *Dead Man* is derived more from one person's imagination than from any person's library.

IV

The notion of what Nobody calls 'passing through the mirror' seems to have a lot to do with the way the movie is structured: not only the industrial town at the beginning and the Makah settlement at the end – the voyage on the train and the voyage in the sea canoe, both periodically punctuated by losses of consciousness and fade-outs – but also throughout Blake and Nobody's trek through the wilderness, when we see practically every location twice, first with them, then with the bounty hunters or

In Machine …

.. and in the Makah
settlement

marshals following behind them. For Jarmusch this device has to do with 'that abstract idea that Nobody has to pass Blake through this mirror of water and send him back to the spirit level of the world'.

As indicated earlier, this practice of looking at the same thing in different ways, analogous in some ways to the repetition of certain images and rhymes in a poem, can be viewed as the principle behind most of Jarmusch's previous work. (A characteristic example is the three escaped prisoners of *Down by Law* discovering, after coming upon a hut in the Louisiana woods, that the bunk beds are similar to those in their former prison cell.)

V

As an acid Western, belonging mainly to a cinematic subgenre, *Dead Man* in some ways goes beyond all the predecessors cited in Chapter 6 in formulating a chilling, savage frontier poetry to justify its hallucinated agenda and its laconic form of magical realism. But in other respects, Blake's westbound journey with Nobody also falls into a classic literary pattern found in some of the most famous American novels: a biracial male couple bonding, escaping civilisation together and moving back towards innocence, a pattern famously outlined by Leslie Fiedler in what is probably his most influential essay:

What ... do all these books [including Dana's *Two Years Before the Mast*, Cooper's Leather-stocking Novels, *Moby Dick*, and *Huckleberry Finn*] have in common? As boys' books we should expect them shyly, guiltlessly as it were, to proffer a chaste male love as the ultimate emotional experience – and this is spectacularly the case. In Dana, it is the narrator's melancholy love for the *kanaka*, Hope; in Cooper, the lifelong affection of Natty Bumppo and Chingachgook; in Melville, Ishmael's love for Queequeg; in Twain, Huck's feeling for Nigger Jim. As the focus of emotion, where we are accustomed to find in the world's great novels some heterosexual passion, be it 'platonic' love or adultery, seduction, rape, or long-drawn-out flirtation, we come instead on the fugitive slave and the no-account boy lying side by side on a raft borne by the endless river toward an impossible escape, or the pariah sailor waking in the tattooed arms of the brown harpooner on the verge of their impossible quest.[38]

Admittedly, Blake and Nobody both have bouts of heterosexual passion (although the first of these is quickly followed by the woman's death and the second is rudely interrupted by Blake), and I don't mean to imply that *Dead Man* is merely a closeted version of something like Andy Warhol's *Lonesome Cowboys* (1968). But the homoerotic links between the two leading characters can't be denied either; and the movement away from civilisation and its corruptions and towards innocence and purity implied in Fiedler's analysis can be certainly felt in the passage of Blake from Machine to the Makah village.

Yet however classically literary the ingredients of *Dead Man* might be, their realisation places them in a realm that is finally extra-literary, and more provocative as a cultural statement for being so. Emblematic of this status is both the title of Janet Bergstrom's recent anthology *Endless Night: Cinema and Psychoanalysis, Parallel Histories* and the beginning of her introduction:

The title of this book is taken from a line spoken in Jim Jarmusch's *Dead Man*: 'Some are born to sweet delight, some are born to endless night.' Endless night, that modality of timeless dark wandering, evokes the remarkably material dreamlike search for intelligibility sustained throughout *Dead Man* without ever being thematized as such or, indeed, as any identifiable state. *Endless Night* seems to me an appropriate designation for this collection of essays, since psychoanalysis and film theory, both, are drawn to the darkness in their quest for logics of meaning.[39]

Bergstrom is, of course, perfectly aware that the title of her collection originates with William Blake and not with Jim Jarmusch. Yet the fact that she none the less chooses to credit *Dead Man* rather than *Songs of Experience* for her inspiration is surely indicative of the kind of resonance it has for her and some other viewers. Which is another way of saying that the film is haunted by literature in much the same way that the Americas are haunted by the slaughter of Native Americans. The process by which Blake the poet of the late eighteenth century is made to speak for another tribe a century later also enables him to become a shaman for us all yet another century after the action of *Dead Man*: radically decontextualised and then just as radically recontextualised, the words of a great writer continue to speak after traversing continents as well as several lifetimes, reappearing as the English translation of an otherwise lost language, an ignored and forgotten tongue. As Jarmusch sees it, that may be the only way that some kinds of literature can survive in the present – by finding a new kind of use value.

8 Closure

The end is important in all things.
Yamamoto Tsunetomo, *Hagakure: The Book of the Samurai* (quoted in *Ghost Dog*)

When we speak of 'seriousness' in fiction ultimately we are talking about an attitude toward death.
Thomas Pynchon

One doesn't ordinarily think of Jarmusch as a religious film-maker, but it might be argued that all his films have a spiritual as well as philosophical dimension. However one interprets *Dead Man*, it's difficult not to read it as some sort of apocalyptic statement – not only because intimations about genocidal loss inform it at every turn, but also because just about every character in it whom we're able to care about dies before the end. (The only exceptions are on the train, in Machine, and in the Makah village; everywhere else in the film winds up as a massive graveyard.)

Whether or not *Dead Man* can actually be categorised as millennial, it certainly calls to mind that mode if only because its journey back in historical time also suggests a certain forward motion evocative of science fiction, and because the overall movement in both directions suggests something terminal about the direction of narrative itself. For a movie that begins and ends in metaphor, it's a logical progression. Describing a

A millennial ending?

voyage to the furthest point west, running parallel to a death trip that in Nobody's terms is also a return to origins, the film ends with a wide expanse of cavernous sky and ocean conceived as an empty stage. If there's anything like a curtain speech, we have to deliver it ourselves, to the strains of Neil Young's music.

Appendix
Aside on Authorship and Methods of Composition

A strange, poetic monologue on the train by the man who stokes the
engine's fire (Crispin Glover) simultaneously prefigures the film's final
sequence (while conjuring up water to 'go with' the man's fire) and
resembles the sort of stoned rap one can imagine someone delivering in an
earlier Jarmusch film: 'Look out the window. ... Doesn't this remind you
of when you're in the boat and then later that night you're lying, looking
up at the ceiling, and the water in your head was not dissimilar from the
landscape, and you think to yourself, "Why is it that the landscape is
moving, but the boat is still?"'

What such a monologue implies – the inability to distinguish between
inner consciousness and external reality – is carried over in the remainder of
the film with hallucinatory brilliance. Speaking to the bounty hunters in his
office, Dickinson addresses his remarks to a stuffed bear. One of these
bounty hunters (Michael Wincott) sleeps with a teddy bear and muses at one
point, 'Ever wish you were the moon?' When Nobody recounts his capture
as a boy by white men and their manner of displaying him like a zoo animal in
a cage in different cities, he is utterly convinced that 'each time I arrived at
another city, somehow the white men would move their people there ahead
of me. The new city would contain the same white people as the last, and I
could not understand how a whole city of people could be moved so quickly.'
Collectively these images conjure up a crazed version of America at its most
solipsistic, hankering after its own lost origins.

ROSENBAUM: I noticed that the weird monologue delivered by Crispin Glover on
the train doesn't appear in the copy of the script you sent me. You told me
earlier that none of your scripts get beyond their initial drafts because, as you
put it, final versions of scripts are necessary only when you have to show
something to suits; when you wind up owning all your own negatives, as you
do, it's obviously a whole different ballgame. In this case, I'm intrigued by the
rhyme effects between this monologue and the final scene in the film. Was
this speech worked out with Glover during the shooting?

JARMUSCH: Yeah. I wrote something that was sort of abstract and strange, and he said, 'Can I play with this and rewrite it?' I said, 'Please do; let's just go over it before we shoot.'

ROSENBAUM: Had he read the whole script?

JARMUSCH: Yeah, I think he did; he certainly knew the whole story. But he was the one who wrote, 'looking up at the ceiling'. I had a similar line about, 'Why is it that the landscape is moving but the boat is still?' – similar, but not as beautiful as what Crispin wrote. He made it much stronger, and much more interesting, in my opinion.

ROSENBAUM: And you said Michael Wincott wrote many of his lines as well.

JARMUSCH: Yeah, he improvised a lot. He would ask for a theme – like I would say, 'Oh, the sun's setting,' and he'd go away and make shit up.

ROSENBAUM: This seems related to what I find musical about your films. You're like a bandleader who knows when to use something written and when to ask someone to take a solo.

JARMUSCH: Well, you have to know what the actors' strengths are. Some aren't for improvisation and they want the map; others are. I've been reading Miles [Davis]'s autobiography – lately I've been obsessed with the Quintet, mid- to late 60s. Tony Williams was into Ornette [Coleman] and Miles was not, and Miles admits, 'I gotta learn from other cats who come from another style, that's always been my way. I don't tell them what to play. I'm the leader, but only because I orchestrate who's gonna play together.' And that's really important. If I'd written all of Michael Wincott's dialogue, it would be nowhere near as good as what he comes up with, y'know? And Johnny brought a lot of things to the film, although he's an actor who likes to have a map. Gary Farmer brought a lot of things too. That's why I think the whole auteur thing is so ridiculous, because it's a collaboration on every level.

ROSENBAUM: Well, auteurism exists largely for the convenience of critics and other packagers. It's mainly a way of reading movies, not of explaining how they're made. I recall Terry Gilliam speaking last year at a film festival about how he's surrounded by collaborators who think up 'typical Gilliam touches' – many of which he wants to avoid, because he'd rather try something new.

JARMUSCH: I have my friend Drew Kunin, my sound mixer whom I've worked with on every film except *Permanent Vacation*. He's one of my close friends, and many times on a film shoot, in the middle of a scene, I'll ask him for advice and he'll make suggestions. I'm not asking him for technical help about the sound; he's a writer, too, but I've never written anything with him. But it's invaluable to have him there if I need to run something by him. And then there's the editing, which Jay Rabinowitz has a lot to do with as well. I'm pretty dictatorial about it in general, but I also like to leave him alone and let him cut a scene first, without me there. And he has no idea how I designed the thing; it's usually a puzzle to him. So sometimes he'll do something I would never have thought of.

Postscript

When I interviewed Jarmusch about *Down by Law* for *Cahiers du Cinéma* in October 1986,[40] he made passing allusions to the two features he hoped to make next. One was to be filmed in subdued colour, ideally in winter light (which inspired me to send him a video, unfortunately scanned, of William Wellman's *Track of the Cat* [1954]); whether or not this eventually evolved into *Mystery Train* is something I've never gotten around to asking him. The other project was a black-and-white Western – a project he was planning to make with screenwriter Rudolph Wurlitzer, Tom Waits as the principal character and Robby Müller as cinematographer. Though neither Wurlitzer nor Waits (who worked together on *Candy Mountain* [1987] during this period) remained with this latter project, Müller – who first worked with Jarmusch on *Down by Law*, and has since shot all his features except for *Night on Earth* – remained; and as Jarmusch made clear to me in our 1986 interview, Müller was a significant creative collaborator in helping to map out the visual design of *Down by Law*.

For all the differences between these two beautiful black-and-white features – some of it possibly attributable to the influence of black-and-white Japanese films shot in forests – the particular look of *Dead Man*, a singular feeling for light, smoke and leafy textures, clearly derives in part from that first collaboration.

Notes

1 Roger Ebert, 'Dead Man' – www.suntimes.../ebert/ebert_reviews/1996/06/062801.html

2 For those who'd like to look up the original, Raymond Bellour, Michaux's editor at Gallimard, offers the following: 'La phrase de Michaux mise en exergue à Dead Man se trouve … dans le texte "La nuit des Bulgares," p. 154 de l'édition Gallimard en collection blanche, ou p. 631 du volume I de la Pléiade. Elle va ainsi en français: "Il est toujours préférable de ne pas voyager avec un mort."'

3 Greil Marcus, '[Dead Again]: Here are 10 reasons why Dead Man is the best movie of the end of the 20th century', Salon – www.salon.com/ent/feature/1999/12/02/deaman, 2 December 1999.

4 A particularly egregious instance of this bias can be found in Janet Maslin's final report on the festival in the New York Times (30 May 1999), which devoted roughly twice as much space to Weinstein's angry pronouncements as it did to the prizes or the films that won them. The same sort of bias has been reflected in American TV coverage of the Cannes prizes as well as the Academy Awards, with the cameras frequently poised to record Weinstein's reactions.

5 Kent Jones, 'Dead Man', Cineaste vol. 22 no. 2, 1996, p. 45.

6 See my more extended discussion of this issue in '"New Hollywood" and the 60s Melting Pot', included in Alexander Horwath's collection The Last Great American Picture Show: New Hollywood 1967–1976 (Vienna: Wespennest, 1995), pp. 103–25; English edition forthcoming in 2001 from the University of Amsterdam Press.

7 Quoted in John Pierson, Spike, Mike, Slackers and Dykes: A Guided Tour Across a Decade of American Independent Cinema (New York: Hyperion/Miramax, 1995), p. 32.

8 Tzvetan Todorov, The Conquest of America: The Question of the Other, translated by Richard Howard (New York: Harper & Row, 1984), p. 133.

9 Depp proudly displays this tattoo in a recent issue of a popular French movie magazine. See 'Johnny Depp par Johnny Depp', edited and photographed by Christophe d'Yvoire, Studio Magazine, February 2000, p. 98.

10 Tag Gallagher, 'Angels Gambol Where They Will: John Ford's Indians', Film Comment, September–October 1993. Reprinted in Jim Kitses and Gregg Rickman (eds), The Western Reader (New York: Limelight Editions, 1998), p. 274.

11 Ward Churchill, Fantasies of the Master Race (San Francisco: City Lights Books, 1998); Jacquelyn Kilpatrick, Celluloid Indians: Native Americans and Film (Lincoln and London: University of Nebraska Press, 1999).

12 Churchill, Fantasies of the Master Race, p. 167.

13 Ibid., p. 203.

14 Kilpatrick, Celluloid Indians, pp. 169, 176.

15 Gallagher, 'Angels Gambol', p. 269.

16 Lesley Stern, 'White Man', in The Smoking Book (Chicago and London: University of Chicago Press, 1999), pp. 42, 44. Stern includes a brief paragraph about Dead Man (p. 43).

17 Thomas Colbath and Stephen Blush, 'Jim Jarmusch Interview', Seconds Magazine no. 37 – http://members.tripod.com~jimjarmusch/sec96.html, 1996.

18 These music credits come respectively from David Meeker's Jazz in the Movies (London: British Film Institute, 1972), p. 4 and Nicole Brenez's Shadows (Paris: Editions Nathan, 1995), p. 45.

19 Marcus, '[Dead Again]'.

20 Colbath and Blush, 'Jim Jarmusch Interview'.

21 J. Hoberman, 'Promised Lands', *Village Voice*, 14 May 1996.

22 Adrian Martin, transcript of broadcast review of *Dead Man* on *This Week in Film*, Radio National (Australia), 20 April 1996.

23 A 1973 restoration in re-edited form of the 1914 film, *In the Land of the Head-Hunters*.

24 Todd J. Tubutis, 'Filming a Makah Village for Jim Jarmusch's *Dead Man*', unpublished MA thesis submitted to the Department of Anthropology and Sociology, University of British Columbia, July 1998, pp. 35–6, 39.

25 Cited in Richard Poirier, *The Performing Self* (New York: Oxford University Press, 1971), p. 23.

26 For a more detailed discussion of this subject, see my article, 'The Countercultural Histories of Rudy Wurlitzer', *Written By* vol. 2 no.11, November 1998, pp. 40–5.

27 Gregg Rickman, 'The Western Under Erasure: *Dead Man*', in Kitses and Rickman (eds), *The Western Reader*, pp. 381–404 (see footnote 10).

28 Gayatri Chakravorty Spivak, Translator's Preface to Jacques Derrida, *Of Grammatology* (Baltimore and London: The Johns Hopkins University Press, 1976), p. xiv.

29 J. Hoberman and Jonathan Rosenbaum, *Midnight Movies*, 2nd edn (New York: Da Capo Press, 1992), p. 228.

30 Rickman, 'The Western Under Erasure', p. 401.

31 Phillip Lopate, 'The Last Taboo', in Katherine Washburn and John Thornton (eds), *Dumbing Down: Essays on the Strip-Mining of American Culture* (New York and London: W. W. Norton, 1996), p. 168.

32 William Troy, 'Notes on *Finnegans Wake*', in Stanley Edgar Hyman (ed.), *William Troy: Selected Essays* (New Brunswick, NJ: Rutgers University Press, 1967), p. 97.

33 Included in *Movies as Politics* (Berkeley: University of California Press, 1997), pp. 183–94.

34 Phillip Lopate, 'In Search of the Centaur: The Essay-Film', *The Threepenny Review* no. 48, Winter 1992, pp. 20–8.

35 Jones, '*Dead Man*', p. 46.

36 Northrop Frye, 'Blake's Introduction to Experience', in Frye (ed.), *Blake: A Collection of Critical Essays* (Englewood Cliffs, NJ: Prentice-Hall, 1966), p. 24.

37 Rickman, 'The Western Under Erasure', p. 382.

38 Leslie Fiedler, 'Come Back to the Raft Ag'in, Huck Honey!', originally published in 1948; reprinted in *An End to Innocence* (New York: Stein and Day, 1972), pp. 144–5.

39 Janet Bergstrom, 'Introduction: Parallel Lines', in *Endless Night: Cinema and Psychoanalysis, Parallel Histories* (Berkeley: University of California Press, 1999), p. 1.

40 Jonathan Rosenbaum, 'Pour quitter quelque chose: entretien avec Jim Jarmusch', *Cahiers du Cinéma* no. 389, November 1986, p. 50.

Credits

DEAD MAN

USA/Germany/Japan
1995

Director
Jim Jarmusch
Producer
Demetra J. MacBride
Screenplay
Jim Jarmusch
Director of Photography
Robby Müller
Editor
Jay Rabinowitz
Production Designer
Robert Ziembicki
Music/Music Performer
Neil Young

©12-Gauge Productions, Inc.
Production Companies
Pandora Film, JVC and
Newmarket Capital Group,
L. P. present
a 12-Gauge production
This motion picture was
made as a co-production
with Pandora Film, Frankfurt
and with the support of FFA
Berlin Filmboard Berlin-
Brandenburg/Filmstiftung
NRW
Co-producer
Karen Koch
Production Manager
Beth DePatie
**Production Executive
(Germany)**
Michael Boehme/Camera
Film

Production Co-ordinator
Jennifer Roth
**Assistant Production
Co-ordinators**
Robert W. Davis,
Exile Ramirez
**New York Office
Co-ordinator**
Carol Abady
Location Manager
Martha C. Pilcher
**Assistant Location
Manager**
Birgit Staudt
Arizona Location Liaison
P. J. Connolly
**Post-production
Co-ordination**
Birgit Staudt, Carol Abady
Production Accountant
Gwendolyn Everman
**Assistant Production
Accountant**
Whitney J. Willard
**Post-production
Accountant**
Danielle Sotet
**Production Office
Assistants**
David Matson, Robin Bursey,
Jean Michel Dissard,
Betsy Everman
**Key Set Production
Assistant**
Patrick Fuchs
Set Production Assistants
Sam Hyde, Jeffrey
Seymann, Hildegard
Bongarts
Hangin'-out Guy
Nemo Labrizzi

Mr Depp's Assistant
Christi Dembrowski
1st Assistant Director
Todd Pfeiffer
2nd Assistant Director
Judy Gorjanc
**2nd Second Assistant
Director**
Connie Maverick
Script Supervisor
Tricia Ronten
Casting
Ellen Lewis, Laura Rosenthal
Casting Assistant
Ali Farrell
Extras Casting
Arizona:
Sunny Seibel
Nevada:
Nevada Casting Group
Oregon:
Linda Lee/Total Look Talent
Makah Tribe:
Donna Wilkie
**Second Unit Director of
Photography**
Cris Lombardi
First Assistant Camera
Tim Tjujerman
Second Unit:
Kate Butler
Second Assistant Camera
Lisa Ferguson
Steadicam Operators
Kirk Gardner, David
Luckenbach, Robert
Gorelick, Jeff Mart
Steadicam Assistants
Emil Hampton, Joe Thibo,
Julian Whatley,
Brian Bernstein

Key Grips
Robert K. Feldmann
Second Unit:
Charles Smith
Best Boy Grip
Byron McCulloch
Dolly Grip
Ken Davis
Grips
Eric Budlong, Tony Pirri,
Bobby L. Smith
Gaffer
Christopher Porter
Best Boy Electric
Michael Palmer
Electricians
Todd Heater, Jon Hokanson,
James E. Brisbin
Greensmen
Kenneth Stellar,
Michael Bennett
Still Photographer
Christine Parry
Stills Intern
Christian Bongers
Digital Visual Effects
R/Greenberg Associates
West, Inc. A division of R/GA
Digital Studios
Visual Effects Supervisor:
Jon Farhat
Producer:
Steven T. Puri
Production Co-ordinator:
Anne Putnam
Additional Compositing
Pacific Title & Art Studio,
Ken Smith
Pacific Title Digital,
Joe Gareri

Visual Effects
Balsmeyer & Everett, Inc.
Visual Effects Supervisor:
Randall Balsmeyer
Digital Compositing:
Daniel Leung
Special Effects
Co-ordinator
FTS Effects/Lou Carlucci
Special Effects Assistant
John Carlucci
Special Effects Animation
The Effects House,
Don Nolan
First Assistant Editor
Tony Grocki
Assistant Editors
Jennifer Apel, Anne O'Brien
Art Director
Ted Berner
Art Department
Co-ordinator
Elizabeth A. Beckman
Set Decorator
Dayna Lee
Lead Scenic Artist
Craig A. Muzio
Scenics
George 'Alex' Fleming,
Cheyenne Ali,
Kenneth Sylvester
Leadman
Rick Lambert
On-set Dresser
Kevin Hughes
Swing Gang
Tony Gibson, John A. Foote,
Karen Clark
Totem Pole Carvers
Greg Colfax, Ernie Cheeka

Construction
Co-ordinator
Bill Holmquist
Construction Foreman
Arthur Allyn
Carpenter Foreman
Terry Kempf
Carpenters
Mark Balda, Michael Blair,
Mark Borg, Walter Milkowski,
Jack Orlando,
Jim Stephenson
Property Master
John C. Pattison
2nd Assistant Prop
Master
Suzanne LaPick
3rd Assistant Props
Edie Douglass
Costume Designer
Marit Allen
Assistant Costume
Designer
Abram Waterhouse
Costume Supervisor
Susie Money
Costumer
Birgitta Bjerke
On-set Costumer
Paul A. Simmons, jun.
Native American Costume
Maker
David Powell
Seamstress
Suzanne Bantit
Stitcher
Raquel Stewart
Key Make-up
Neal Martz
Assistant Make-up
Todd Kleitsch

Mr Depp's Make-up
Patty York
Prosthetic Effects
Steve Johnson's XFX
Effects Production Co-
ordinator:
Joe Fordham
Effects Project Manager:
Mark Habegger
Prosthetics:
Richard Alonzo, Leon
Laderach, David DuPuis
Mold Maker:
Brent Baker
Foam Technician:
Tom Irvin
Key Hairstylist
Scott W. Farley
Mr Depp's Hair
Claire Corsick
Titles Designed and
Produced by
Balcmeyer & Everett, Inc.
Timer
Tom Salvatore
Music Production
L. A. Johnson
Music Executive
Elliot Rabinowitz
Musical Score Recording
Engineer
John Hanlon
Musical Score Recording
Services
Le Mobile, Guy
Charbonneau, Charlie Bouis,
Eric Johnston
Musical Score Production
Services
Tim Foster, Arthur Rosato,
Sal Trentin, Louis Grappi

Redwood Digital
John Nowland,
John Hausmann
Sound Mixer
Drew Kunin
Additional Sound
Recordists
Coll Anderson,
Stacey Tanner
Re-recording Engineer
Dominick Tavella
Mix Re-recordists
Keith Culbertson, Hextro
Supervising Sound
Editor
Robert Hein
Assistant Sound Editors
Julie Lindner,
Daniel Evans Farkas
Apprentice Sound Editor
Kimberly R. McCord
Boom Operator
Mark Goodermote
Dialogue Editor
Sylvia Menno
Effects Editors
Eugene Gearty, Magdaline
Volaitis
Foley
Supervisor:
Bruce Pross
Artist:
Marko Costanzo
Editors:
Frank Kern, Kam Chan
Mr Depp's Stand-in
Bruce Corkum
Mr Farmer's Stand-in
Gilbert Manygoats
Projectionist
David Graham

Dailies Projectionist
Alan Burke
Dailies Supervisors
Don Donigi, Steve Blakely
Cultural Consultant
Kathy Whitman
Canoe Technical Adviser
Kevin S. Colley
Animal Wranglers
Red Wolverton,
Kip Wolverton,
Holly H. Edwards,
Margory Wolverton
Elk Wrangler
Jeffrey King
Transportation
Co-ordinator
Antonio Molina
Transportation Captain
Craig Williams
Honeywagon Driver
Don Martin
Mr Depp's Driver
Buck Holland
Swing Driver
Dale Dodds
Construction Driver
Felipe Gallego
Drivers
John Ray Floyd,
Jolene Floyd, Bill Getzwiller,
Jeffrey M. Landis, Jeff Lira,
Jan Lyons, Mary Martin,
Harry McCrorey, Laree
Scrignolli, Brian Steagall,
Fred G. Steagall,
Jack H. Swauger,
Chandler Vinar
Safety Divers
Matt Roberts,
Watson Devore

Boat Captains
Randy Court, Mike Gibson
Makah Canoe Skipper
Harry McCarty
Medics
Arizona:
Mike McNally
Oregon/California:
Diane Carlucci
Craft Service
Sioux Dean, Danielle
LaClare
Catering
DeLuxe Catering,
Rick Eggers, Jordan Faeth,
Ken Weintraub
Production Legal Advisor
Richard B. Heller, Esq.,
Frankfurt, Garbus, Klein & Selz
Foreign Sales Agent
CiBy Sales
Production Insurance
RHH-Albert G. Ruben
Insurance, George Walden,
Steve Carroll
Completion Bond by
Film Finances, Inc.,
Nordstern (Germany)
Dollies by
Leonard Chapman,
J. L. Fischer
Camera Equipment by
Otto Nemenz International
Cameras
Moviecam, Arriflex
Film Stock
Kodak (Berlin)
Film Laboratory
DuArt Film Laboratories,
New York
Sound Facilities
Sound One Corporation, C-5

**Lightworks Editing System
provided by**
Tribeca Henninger Editing
Tools

Neil Young performs
courtesy of Warner Brothers
Records

Cast
Johnny Depp
William Blake
Gary Farmer
Nobody
Lance Henriksen
Cole Wilson
Michael Wincott
Conway Twill
Mili Avital
Thel Russell
Iggy Pop
Salvatore 'Sally' Jenko
Billy Bob Thornton
Big George Drakoulious
Jared Harris
Benmont Tench
Crispin Glover
train fireman
Eugene Byrd
Johnny 'The Kid' Pickett
Michelle Thrush
Nobody's girlfriend
Jimmie Ray Weeks
Marvin, older marshal
Mark Bringelson
Lee, younger marshal
Gabriel Byrne
Charlie Dickinson
John Hurt
John Scholfield
Alfred Molina
trading post missionary

Robert Mitchum
John Dickinson
Gibby Haines
man with gun in alley
George Duckworth
man at end of street
Richard Boes
man with wrench
John North
Mr Olafsen
Peter Schrum
drunk
Thomas Bettles
first young Nobody
Daniel Chas Stacy
second young Nobody
Mike Dawson
old man with wanted posters
John Pattison
1st man at trading post
Todd Pfeiffer
2nd man at trading post
Leonard Bowechop
Cecil Cheeka
Michael McCarty
Makah villagers

10,827 feet
120 minutes
[134 at Cannes premiere]
Dolby stereo
Black and White

Locations
Segments of the film were
shot on location within the
Coconino National Forest,
Sedona and Peaks Ranger
Districts, Arizona

Credits compiled by Markku
Salmi, BFI Filmographic Unit

Bibliography

Bergstrom, Janet (ed.), *Endless Night: Cinema and Psychoanalysis, Parallel Histories* (Berkeley: University of California Press, 1999).

Brenez, Nicole, *Shadows* (Paris: Editions Nathan, 1995).

Burroughs, William S., *Naked Lunch* (New York: Grove Press, 1959).

Churchill, Ward, *Fantasies of the Master Race* (San Francisco: City Lights Books, 1998).

Colbath, Thomas and Stephen Blush, 'Jim Jarmusch Interview', *Seconds Magazine* no. 37 [http://members.tripod.com/~jimjarmusch/sec96.html], 1996.

Ebert, Roger, '*Dead Man*' [www.suntimes.com/ebert/ebert_reviews/1996/06/062801.html]

Fiedler, Leslie, 'Come Back to the Raft Ag'in, Huck Honey!', in *An End to Innocence* (New York: Stein and Day, 1972).

Frye, Northrop, 'Blake's Introduction to Experience', in Frye (ed.), *Blake: A Collection of Critical Essays* (Englewood Cliffs, N.I: Prentice-Hall, 1966), pp. 23–31.

Gallagher, Iag, 'Angels Gambol Where They Will: John Ford's Indians', *Film Comment*, September–October 1993.

Hoberman, J., 'Promised Lands', *Village Voice*, 14 May 1996.

—— and Jonathan Rosenbaum, *Midnight Movies*, 2nd edn (New York: Da Capo Press, 1992).

Jones, Kent, '*Dead Man*', *Cineaste* vol. 22 no. 2, 1996, pp. 45–6.

Kazin, Alfred (ed.), *The Portable Blake* (New York: The Viking Press, 1946).

Kilpatrick, Jacquelyn, *Celluloid Indians: Native Americans and Film* (Lincoln and London: University of Nebraska Press, 1999).

Lopate, Phillip, 'In Search of the Centaur: The Essay-Film', *The Threepenny Review* no. 48, Winter 1992.

—— 'The Last Taboo', in Katherine Washburn and John Thornton (eds), *Dumbing Down: Essays on the Strip-Mining of American Culture* (New York and London: W. W. Norton, 1996).

Marcus, Greil, '[Dead Again]: Here are ten reasons why *Dead Man* is the best movie of the end of the 20th century', *Salon* [www.salon.com/ent/feature/1999/12/02/deadman], 2 December 1999.

Martin, Adrian, transcript of broadcast review of *Dead Man* on *This Week in Film*, Radio National (Australia), 20 April 1996.

Meeker, David, *Jazz in the Movies* (London: British Film Institute, 1972).

Poirier, Richard, *The Performing Self* (New York: Oxford University Press, 1971).

Rickman, Gregg, 'The Western Under Erasure: *Dead Man*', in Jim Kitses and Rickman (eds), *The Western Reader* (New York: Limelight Editions, 1998), pp. 381–404.

Rosenbaum, Jonathan, 'Pour quitter quelque chose: entretien avec Jim Jarmusch', *Cahiers du Cinéma* no. 389, November 1986.

—— '"New Hollywood" and the 60s Melting Pot', in Alexander Howarth (ed.), *The Last Great American Picture Show: New Hollywood 1967–1976* (Vienna: Wespennest, 1995), pp. 103–25; English edition forthcoming in 2001 from the University of Amsterdam Press.

—— *Movies as Politics* (Berkeley: University of California Press, 1997).

—— 'The Countercultural Histories of Rudy Wurlitzer', *Written By* vol. 2 no. 11, November 1998, pp. 40–5.

Spivak, Gayatri Chakravorty, Translator's Preface to Jacques Derrida, *Of Grammatology* (Baltimore and London: The Johns Hopkins University Press, 1976).

Stern, Lesley, *The Smoking Book* (Chicago and London: University of Chicago Press, 1999).

Todorov, Tzvetan, *The Conquest of America: The Question of the Other*, translated by Richard Howard (New York: Harper & Row, 1984).

Tubutis, Todd J., 'Filming a Makah Village for Jim Jarmusch's *Dead Man*', unpublished MA thesis submitted to the Department of Anthropology and Sociology, The University of British Columbia, July 1998.

Also Published

L'Argent
Kent Jones (1999)

Blade Runner
Scott Bukatman (1997)

Blue Velvet
Michael Atkinson (1997)

Caravaggio
Leo Bersani & Ulysse Dutoit
(1999)

Crash
Iain Sinclair (1999)

The Crying Game
Jane Giles (1997)

Don't Look Now
Mark Sanderson (1996)

Easy Rider
Lee Hill (1996)

The Exorcist
Mark Kermode (1997,
2nd edn 1998)

Independence Day
Michael Rogin (1998)

Last Tango in Paris
David Thompson (1998)

**Once Upon a Time in
America**
Adrian Martin (1998)

Pulp Fiction
Dana Polan (2000)

The Right Stuff
Tom Charity (1997)

**Saló or The 120 Days of
Sodom**
Gary Indiana (2000)

Seven
Richard Dyer (1999)

The Terminator
Sean French (1996)

Thelma & Louise
Marita Sturken (2000)

The Thing
Anne Billson (1997)

**The 'Three Colours'
Trilogy**
Geoff Andrew (1998)

Titanic
David M. Lubin (1999)

The Wings of the Dove
Robin Wood (1999)

**Women on the Verge of a
Nervous Breakdown**
Peter William Evans (1996)

**WR – Mysteries of the
Organism**
Raymond Durgnat (1999)

Forthcoming

Do the Right Thing
Ed Guerrero (2001)

Star Wars
Peter Wollen (2001)

BFI Modern Classics combine careful research with high-quality writing about contemporary cinema.

If you would like to receive further information about future **BFI Modern Classics** or about other books from BFI Publishing, please fill in your name and address and return this card to us:*
(No stamp required if posted in the UK, Channel Islands, or Isle of Man.)

NAME

ADDRESS

POSTCODE

WHICH **BFI MODERN CLASSIC** DID YOU BUY?

* In North America, please return your card to: Indiana
University Press, 601 N. Morton Street,
Bloomington, IN 47404, USA

BFI Publishing
21 Stephen Street
FREEPOST 7
LONDON
W1E 4AN